THE GAME OF
BILLIARDS

THE GAME OF BILLIARDS

Clive Cottingham, Jr.

WITH DRAWINGS BY ED VEBELL

AND DIAGRAMS BY JOHN H. PFISTER

BARNES & NOBLE BOOKS
A DIVISION OF HARPER & ROW, PUBLISHERS
New York, Cambridge, Philadelphia, San Francisco
London, Mexico City, São Paulo, Sydney

A hardcover edition of this book was published by J. B. Lippincott Company.

First BARNES & NOBLE BOOKS edition published 1984.

Library of Congress Cataloging in Publication Data

Cottingham, Clive.
   The game of billiards.

   Reprint. Originally published: Philadelphia : Lippincott, 1964.
   1. Billiards. I. Title.
GV891.C72 1984   794.7′2   83-49019
ISBN 0-06-464087-6 (pbk.)

84   85   86   87   88   10   9   8   7   6   5   4   3   2   1

To those who enjoy billiards

CONTENTS

Part One

AN INTRODUCTION TO BILLIARDS

Part Two

BILLIARDS FOR BEGINNERS

CONTENTS

Part Three

ADVANCED SHOTS

CONTENTS

Part Four

THE DIAMOND SYSTEM
FOR THREE-CUSHION BILLIARDS

PART ONE

An Introduction to Billiards

1

"A most genteel, cleanly and ingenious game"

THE COMPLEAT GAMESTER, 1674

THE ANCIENT and honored game of billiards is enjoying a great revival everywhere in the world. Nine thousand new billiard parlors were built in Japan alone in a single year. The English are at the billiard tables by the thousands, and so are the French, the Danes, the Swiss, the Australians, and the New Zealanders. Here in America the game is enjoying a tremendous surge of popularity.

Billiards has acquired a "new look" through the use of glamorous surroundings and brightly colored tables which have made it a fashionable pastime again, as it was in its heyday at the turn of the century. Builders of luxury homes are putting in billiard rooms as adjuncts to, or substitutes for, the familiar rumpus room. Entire families are gathering round the billiard table in a new expression of "togetherness."

Sales of billiard tables, cues, and balls have more than doubled in the past year or two in this country, principally as a result of the opening of modern parlors, designed along the lines of bowling lanes and aimed at giving the game a new image, completely different from the atmosphere of the old-time pool hall.

Gone are the dingy mahogany tables, each lit by a single bulb hanging from the ceiling, and the familiar green baize cloth tops. In their place are dramatically designed Formica or Fiberglas tables with surfaces of blue, tangerine, brown, or beige, in rooms with wall-to-wall carpeting of pastel shades. The air-conditioned interior prevents the accumulation of cigarette-smoke haze. Soundproof ceilings and walls reduce noise to a minimum. Indirect lighting bathes the billiard room, which may contain as many as 40 or 50 tables for both pocket billiards and the three-cushion carom game, in a soft but adequate glow of light. One such establishment in New York employs exotic hostesses (a Chinese, a Cuban, an Indo-Chinese, an Italian, and an Iranian) to usher customers to their tables and set up racks of balls.

THE GAME OF BILLIARDS

The revival of interest in billiards probably can be traced to the exposure of hundreds of thousands of servicemen to the pastime during World War II, in training camps and in rest areas overseas. But the recent boom in the sales of equipment and the opening of new parlors can be attributed directly to the phenomenal appeal of the motion picture, *The Hustler*, which portrayed Jackie Gleason and Paul Newman in the role of pool sharks. These actors fascinated audiences the world over with their skilled performances at the billiard table (supervised by the world pocket billiards champion, Willie Mosconi, who was the film's technical adviser.)

Although the motion picture emphasized the tawdry aspect of the game, at the same time it struck a deep chord in the public at large, stimulating a great revival of interest among some 20 million Americans and many millions more abroad. Many of the new enthusiasts of the game are girls and women, who show a natural aptitude for handling a billiard cue. The delicacy of touch, perception, muscular coordination, grace, and rhythm required of a billiard player come quite naturally and instinctively to the fair sex. They have responded gratefully to the glamorous atmosphere of the new establishments with such names as "Rack and Cue," "Guys and Dolls," and "The Q Club." Women who once flocked to bowling lanes are now to be found at the billiard parlors, which have opened near supermarkets, commuting railroad stations, and other convenient locations. Proprietors have provided baby-sitting areas, coffee shops, and cafeterias for the convenience of housewives.

Women have played billiards down through the centuries. Mary, Queen of Scots, and her arch-rival, Queen Elizabeth of England, were both accomplished cue wielders. A recent newspaper photograph of the present Queen Mother Elizabeth making a left-handed shot at a table in the Fleet Street Press Club in London attested to her skill (with either hand) at the billiard table.

Celebrities of all sorts have taken to billiards since it became an "in" pastime. One little shop in the Bowery area of Manhattan, which specializes in turning out custom-made cues and handmade balls, numbers among its customers Fred Astaire, Kim Novak, Jack Lemmon, Tony Curtis, and Milton Berle. Producing a custom-built cue is a veritable United Nations effort, since the best butts are fashioned from

Brazilian rosewood, the shafts are made of domestic rock maple, and the cue tips are a special buckhorn, made from antlers of East Indian deer. Ivory tusks from African elephants are preferred for the best billiard balls.

Manufacturers of billiard equipment were taken by surprise by the sudden demand from dealers during the early 60s. They were swamped with orders for tables and cues for home use, and revenue officers were deluged with applications for licenses to operate new billiard parlors. Six major manufacturers are busily turning out regulation-sized tables for billiard parlors at a rate nearly triple their former output. The demand for folding tables for home use, as well as for churches, schools, clubs, fraternity houses, and other institutions, has increased by nearly 1,000 per cent in less than a decade. More than a half million American homes now boast billiard tables, and industry sources estimate that 10,000 billiard centers are now in use throughout the country.

Mickey Mantle, the baseball star, is among the prominent sports figures who have lent their names to (and invested financially in) chains of billiard lounges—as they did a few years ago with bowling lanes. Many bowling establishments have put in billiard tables, and not a few have converted completely from bowling to billiards.

It is not difficult to discern the reasons for the return of billiards to its former place in American life, before the distractions of radio and television tended to make observers and listeners, rather than active participants, of most of us. In the McKinley and Theodore Roosevelt eras the billiard room in the White House was a busy spot, and such well-known cue devotees as Mark Twain were frequent visitors at presidential billiard sessions.

Billiards is a fascinating and thoroughly demanding game which can be played by people of all ages in pleasant surroundings, by day or by night, and at all times of the year. It has a simplicity which attracts the young. At the same time it can be as exacting as chess and as rewarding as climbing the Matterhorn. In its upper reaches it requires the utmost in imagination and adroitness.

People who play billiards are the fortunate "millionaires" of the sports world. Each player has a little piece of life to himself and a big slice of pleasure. Once he "feels the ivories" or hears the resounding *plop* of a ball falling into a pocket he becomes a different person. The game can bring about a personality change that would take a psychiatrist to fathom. If you are a mouse in the office, you may become a tiger at the table; if you are a dreamer by nature, you become a hard-boiled realist in the billiard lounge. You may not be a striking success in your daily endeavors, but you can compensate by achieving skill at billiards which makes your workaday problems seem smaller.

The renaissance of billiards has coincided with man's entrance into the Space Age. The qualities which produce qualified astronauts and jet pilots are also characteristic of the good billiard player. This has been demonstrated by the use of specially designed circular billiard tables to help train fighter pilots for the U.S. armed forces.

A U.S. Navy flight surgeon, Captain J. A. Niforopulos (who was pocket billiard champion of the Armed Forces during the last world war), and a Texas mathematics professor, Dr. Robert D. Perry, have pointed out the psychological and physiological affinity between billiards and military jet flying. Both activities require a spirit of competition, the will to excell and to win; provide the thrill of executing a maneuver and of hitting a target; and put a premium on the ability to foresee difficulties, on the exercise of good judgment and on the ability to perform under duress with a maximum of self-control. On the physical side, both jet pilots and billiard players need good muscular coordination, good eyesight, good general health, and a good sense of equilibrium.

Captain Niforopulos and Dr. Perry found that a circular table six feet in diameter, with five pockets, was better adapted to the training of future jet pilots than the standard, rectangular, six-pocket billiard table. In their analogy between jet flight and billiards in a circle, the player represents the pilot, the cue represents the control stick in the aircraft, the force of impact on the cue ball represents the throttle, the curved and straight trajectories of the ball on the round table represent the course of the aircraft, and the object balls and the pockets represent the targets.

Oddly enough, the idea of a circular billiards table had occurred to Lewis Carroll, the gifted English writer and mathematician, more than a century before Niforopulos and Perry. (Billiards has frequently fascinated mathematicians and physicists.)

Carroll built such a table while he was teaching mathematics at Oxford University and wrote a two-page leaflet explaining his rules for playing the game which has become a collector's item.

Carroll was also fascinated by the notion of playing billiards within a cube and worked out mathematical problems involving the bouncing of a ball inside rectangular boxes. The idea of playing billiards inside a cubical table is not entirely fanciful in this space age, as the *Scientific American* noted.

"With gigantic space stations perhaps only a few decades away it takes no great prophetic ability to foresee a variety of three-dimensional sports that will take advantage of zero gravity," the magazine pointed out. "Pool adapts neatly to a rectangular room with cushion walls, floor and ceiling, corner pockets and balls numbered from 1 to 35. . . . Of course, there would be difficulties. Air resistance offers much less friction than the felt surface of a pool table . . . it would be hard to keep out of the way of balls flying about in random directions."

But most of us are content to leave the space flights to the Glenns, the Gagarins, and the other astronauts. We will gladly get our thrills of accomplishment on earth and, more specifically, at the billiard table.

Some people, by physical endowment and emotional make-up, are better adapted to individual sports such as billiards than others. But with application and proper guidance in the fundamentals, the average person can become a satisfyingly accomplished billiards player. Needless to say, the better you become at the game, the more rewarding it becomes. You can take it up at any stage of life with the knowledge that a reasonable amount of time spent in studying and practicing will produce worthwhile results. It is a pastime that appeals to all classes of people—shipping clerks and shipowners, businessmen and bakers, physicians and bus drivers, schoolboys and residents of retirement homes.

If you play billiards, why not play well? There are no real shortcuts to success in any field. You must learn the basic foundation of the game slowly in order to avoid being a flashy player with unsound style and grasp of the game. But the rewards for a little fundamental ground-work are awaiting you. You will play better, win more often, and enjoy the game more.

There is nothing mysterious about billiards, but there are many "trade secrets" which have been worked out and proven. These are presented in this book for your use. They are sound, scientific principles that anyone of average intelligence can comprehend. To put them to the test on the table requires only moderate effort.

Many people make a fundamental mistake in going only so far—and not far enough—in their practicing and study of billiards, and they remain mediocre players. Persevere, learn from the experts, be patient, and practice until the mental and mechanical becomes almost automatic—then practice some more. A sound background in billiards will help you eliminate many errors and faults in your game which normally plague the tyro. But no one can eliminate all his or her faults, and the game itself will present certain difficulties which will continually challenge and taunt you. Therein lies its great fascination.

2

A Short History of the Game

BILLIARDS has been fascinating its devotees for a long time, but not so long as some people, notably Shakespeare, would have you believe. The Bard was strong on plot and meter but woefully weak when it came to historical authenticity. His anachronisms were frequent and flagrant. He described clocks striking in Rome during the reign of Julius Caesar, when sun dials were all the rage and mechanical timepieces still centuries off. So too, in *Antony and Cleopatra*, Shakespeare put these words in the mouth of his royal heroine:

"Let's to billiards: come, Charmian."

This tells us only that the game of billiards was being played when Shakespeare wrote the play, in the England of the early seventeenth century. Researchers of the game, including those of the British Museum, have failed to unearth evidence to confirm the existence of billiards in any recognizable form as early as Cleopatra's era. Nor have they been able to verify various tales of billiards seen in the sixth century B.C. by the widely traveled Prince Anacharsis of Scythia, or being played in old Ireland by a king who allegedly left a legacy which included "fifty billiard balls of brass" and cues to match. Billiards, furthermore, would seem to have little resemblance to the ancient games of boula, bouleta, billa, or cum billa.

What it does resemble is the extinct game of pall-mall, popular in England, France, and Italy in the sixteenth century and earlier, from which croquet, hockey, and golf—as well as billiards—probably derived.

Pall-mall was played with a wooden ball four inches in diameter and a curved stick, in an alley. London's fashionable street, Pall Mall, was built on and named for one such alley. Pall-mall players were unhappy when winter weather forced them to interrupt the sport, so they experimented with an indoor version of their pastime. Cramped indoor quarters proved less than satisfactory, however, and frustration flourished until some unsung genius suggested raising the game off the floor and restricting the playing area. This genius might well have been a Frenchman. The name of the game which derived from the raised platform, "billiards" from *bille* or "stick," is French and its earliest enthusiasts and historians were also of that nationality. The game developed rapidly in the great castles and monasteries of medieval France, whose courtiers and monks were also developing handball and the racquet games in the courtyards to while away their leisure hours.

The cachet of the noble and highborn was placed upon the game of billiards from the very beginning. King Henry III was the first of many French monarchs to adopt the sport. He installed a primitive, triangular-shaped table in his chateau at Blois about 1575. The earliest tables were equipped with all manner of obstacles such as hoops or "arches" and pegs. But the French imaginatively simplified and refined "the royal game," as they called it, as they went along.

First of all, guard rails had to be placed around the table to keep the balls from falling off. Rebounds therefore became a new feature of the game. The initial propelling instrument was a kind of mallet, then a mace—a rod with a large end which was placed against the ball. In the course of events, the rod was reversed so that the smaller end was used to propel the ball. This became the modern cue stick. During the reign of Charles IX in 1571, an artist named DeVigne had designed a billiard table with pockets at each corner and one in the center, and had drawn up a code of rules.

Although cues were used as early as 1735 in France, they were rather crude sticks with the striking ends roughened to make firmer contact with the balls. It was not until 1823 that a French player named Mangin got the idea for a leather cue tip. The next step was to apply chalk to the leather tip to prevent slipping.

The first billiard balls were crude, irregular spheres made of stone, leather, or metal. Later ivory was adopted as the ideal material because of its malleability as well as its durability, and in recent years plastics and similar synthetic materials have been used extensively.

The billiard table has undergone many alterations, not only in design but in composition. The original board beds were altered to slate or marble, and eventually felt surfaces were used to cover them. Rubber was added to the inner sides of the table to soften the impact of the ball against the rail boards. The triangular shape was changed to the present rectangle, half as wide as it is long, and six pockets were placed at the corners and sides for the most popular form of the game, pocket billiards.

Billiards was becoming popular at the time the European powers were engaged in the great era of ocean explorations. Many an English, French, Spanish, and Dutch vessel sailing westward over the vast Atlantic expanse carried a billiard table for the amusement of the ship's officers.

The Spaniards are generally credited with introducing the new game to the New World, although this claim might be validly challenged by other nations who were sending explorers to the Western Hemisphere in the post-Columbus movement across the sea. At any rate, the game was so popular in the American colonies that the leading figures of the Revolution, notably Washington and Jefferson, devoted as much of their spare time to the cue as they did their working time to the cause of freedom. The White House always had a billiard room. John Quincy Adams and Abraham Lincoln were among the many presidents who took to the billiard table to seek diversion from the affairs of state.

A major improvement in equipment occurred midway in the nineteenth century, when piano manufacturers began turning out standardized billiard tables. This put the sport on a solid foundation, enabling it to move into its Golden Era of the late 1890s and early 1920s, when every home with any pretension to quality boasted its billiard room and every community with any pretension to size boasted its billiard parlor.

3

Great Billiard Players

OVER THE YEARS the game of billiards has enshrined its own pantheon of heroes, as revered by the followers of the indoor sport as the Babe Ruths, Jack Dempseys, and Red Granges of outdoor sports.

One name must lead all the rest when you speak of the all-time great billiard players—that of the late Willie Hoppe. He was without question the champion's champion. For a half century this courteous genius completely dominated his world, in an era that produced many other great players, from the time when, at eighteen, he defeated the awesome French master, Maurice Vignaux, in an unforgettable series of matches in Paris in 1906 and then captured an incredible number of world titles at three-cushion billiards and balk-line billiards to his death at the age of seventy-one.

I met Willie Hoppe shortly before his death. He was a fine person, vibrant and very much alive, a gentleman of the old school and full of enthusiasm for my interest in his great encounter with Vignaux. His eyes lit up as he recalled his first meeting with the renowned Frenchman, who held the balk-line billiards title of the world for 25 years against all comers. The old master had told the teen-age American to "go out and get a reputation," and Hoppe had done just that by defeating the champion of England.

Three interested Americans were in the large audience in the Palace Hotel when the blond youngster lagged for the first shot with the Lion of France, then in his seventy-third year. They were Willie's father, who had taught him to play at age five; Eddie Foy, an impetuous member of the famed vaudeville family; and Charles M. Schwab, the steel tycoon. The French audience offered odds as high as 7 to 1 that their champion would "roast this duckling." Foy went through the audience taking bets until he ran out of money. Then he prevailed on Schwab "not to sell America short," and the industrialist handed over a fistful of notes to back the American challenger.

The match went badly for Willie Hoppe and his backers at the beginning. The old master had lost none of his finesse. The years had steeled his nerves and confirmed his judgment. He led the tense youngster 130 to 48, and the odds rose to 15 to 1.

"Cover all bets," Schwab told Foy. "We have three days of this. If they beat us tonight we'll catch up with them tomorrow, and the third day we'll cash those tickets."

The partisan audience was hushed and reverent whenever Vignaux was at the table but became noisy and boisterous when Hoppe picked up the cue. Matches flared constantly as people lit up cigars and pipes. The sound of matches striking and the sudden flare of light in the darkness can distract a billiard player sufficiently to cause him to miss a shot. But young Hoppe calmly persevered against the old man and evened the score during the second day of the series.

"Gee, Dad," Willie confided to his father, "I think I can really beat this fellow. He's great, but I feel like David must have felt when he went out to meet Goliath."

On the third day the crowd was in a ferment. Betting odds dropped to 8 to 1 against Hoppe, but the betting was in ten- and twenty-thousand-dollar amounts. The French were eager to bet with Schwab, because they knew his money was good. Foy had long since dropped out, for the betting pace was too hot for him. But Schwab continued to bet on Hoppe, saying, "Win or lose, I am enjoying every moment."

Hoppe went out in front despite the distractions of the unruly audience. The referee finally obtained silence from the crowd by threatening to award the match to the American "unless this nonsense stops." In a sudden rush of respect, Willie completed the contest with a run of 68 and quietly laid his cue on the table. Vignaux, his eyes wet with emotion, was a gallant loser.

"My boy," he told the grinning youngster, "you are the greatest player in the world."

The elder Hoppe sat quietly in his chair, giving a prayer of thanks. Schwab was deluged with congratulations, and Foy was busy collecting their winnings. A new era had been launched in billiards, and for 49 of the next 51 years Willie reigned as champion of the world in some variety of the balk-line, carom, or three-cushion game. Schwab made it a truly memorable day for Willie Hoppe by handing him a gift of $50,000.

Hoppe dominated his sport for 47 years, and when he finally retired, at the age of sixty-five, he had won the astonishing total of 51 world championships and the undisputed title of "Mr. Billiards."

But even in retirement the cue wizard could not remain away from the billiard table, and he continued to give instruction to selected pupils until his death in Miami on February 1, 1959.

Hoppe was one of those rare child prodigies who goes on to fulfill his early promise in maturity. The son of a proprietor of a combination barber shop and pool parlor in Cornwall-on-Hudson, New York, Willie gave his first exhibition at age seven, with his older brother, Frank. Willie was billed as the "Boy Wonder" and, through intense dedication and daily practice, became the world's best balk-line player by the time he was eighteen years old.

Hoppe beat every great player at the various forms of balk-line play, winning dozens of championships from 1906 to 1938. Hoppe and his two closest rivals, Welker Cochran and Young Jake Schaefer, became so proficient at this game that audiences grew bored with their skills, and championship balk-line competition was discontinued. Hoppe then turned to three-cushion billiards, winning his first world title in that variation of the cue sport by defeating Cochran in a Chicago challenge match in 1936. He was unbeaten in 39 consecutive world tournament matches for the next three years, a hot streak unparalleled in the annals of three-cushion competition.

The secret of Hoppe's success was unwavering devotion to the sport and grueling hard work. He once estimated that he had played or practiced billiards four hours a day for 50 years—or the equivalent of 8½ years of continuous play.

While Willie Hoppe was exerting his mastery over the pocketless billiard table, many highly talented players were contesting for top honors in the far more popular game of pocket billiards, or pool. Prominent among these was Ralph Greenleaf, one of the most colorful players of the 1920s.

Greenleaf, tall and handsome, was a glamorous figure who hit the billiard world like a thunderbolt at age seventeen and who was extinguished like a meteor at age forty-seven. He was attractive to women and had a weakness for strong drink. But he had a magic touch at the table which earned him enormous sums during his heyday.

Greenleaf possessed a tremendous arsenal of skill and power. He was a position player with a touch so precise that he could send the ball around the table and have it come to rest within a half-dollar circumference of where he wanted it to stop. He could make the most difficult shots under pressure. He could think his way out of losing games with safety play. He could win and lose gracefully and for more than a decade was the idol of millions. Greenleaf had to be great to withstand the constant pressures from gifted players like Erwin Rudolph, Frank Taberski, Andrew Ponzi, and Onofrio Lauri, who were always ready to topple him. And in the wings, awaiting their turn in the limelight, were Irving Crane and Willie Mosconi, young hopefuls who were destined to set the pocket billiards world afire. (Greenleaf taught the young Mosconi parts of the game, and Willie learned his lessons so well that he easily took over the world championship after Greenleaf.)

Greenleaf combined a great flair for showmanship with tremendous billiards talent. He "played the Palace" on Broadway with a vaudeville routine that earned him $2,000 a week in the days before high taxes. The audience watched him perform trick shots by looking at a huge mirror suspended onstage over the table. He went to Hollywood to make a series of short subjects and was offered an acting contract because of his appeal to women. He chose to continue his billiards career. No other pocket player ever had a greater command of all parts of the game than Greenleaf. He combined the finest stroke, best position, trick shots, coolness under pressure, and showmanship with a great love of the game. People flocked to see him take on the greatest players of his time. In these open tournaments the large 5- by 10-foot tables "looked like putting greens"; the pockets were smaller and the balls larger than ordinary. All this combined to make the game a severe test of skill, yet Greenleaf consistently went through these tournaments to emerge as world champion.

Just one statistic will illustrate how good Greenleaf could be under pressure. In a tournament against 10 of the strongest men in the game, at 125 points per game, Greenleaf missed only 9 called balls in the tournament—9 out of 1,250!

It was not uncommon for Ralph to run 125 points at one turn at the table. One night in Harlem, Greenleaf watched Ponzi run 200 balls and then put his cue down and walk toward the door.

"Where are you going?" Greenleaf asked the erratic Ponzi. "You haven't missed yet, and you just passed the two-hundred mark."

"I'm getting tired of this game," replied Ponzi. "I'm going out for coffee. Take it from here and see what you can do." . .

Ponzi went out, confident that his string would hold Greenleaf for a while. But Greenleaf passed the 300 mark at 3 A.M., and ten minutes later had taken the match with 332 points.

Boxing enthusiasts are fond of arguing over the relative merits of John L. Sullivan and Joe Louis, or Rocky Marciano's hypothetical chances against Jack Dempsey. So billiards enthusiasts ask if Willie Mosconi is as good a pocket billiards player as Ralph Greenleaf at his best. My answer would be an unqualified yes. I have seen Willie in action many times, and I believe he is the greatest pocket billiards player of all time. He has all the qualities of a great champion and has compiled an unequaled record in competition.

I will never forget the first time I saw the immaculate Mosconi at the table. It was in a match against Onofrio Lauri in New York City, and they both put on one of the greatest displays of talent I have ever seen. Lauri had an impressive run of 68 balls on his first turn at the table, but Mosconi ran the game out 125 to 68 in spectacular style. He displayed nerves of steel, the perception of a Botvinnik, a machinelike precision, the catlike grace of Fred Astaire, and the charm of Gentleman Jim Corbett himself. Later I had the privilege of meeting Willie Mosconi personally, and it is a pleasure to report that he is just as much a champion off the billiard table as he is with a cue stick in hand.

Mosconi is a tremendous competitor and a relentless taskmaster. He has enormous pride in his game and constantly struggles for perfection. For 15 years he stayed on top, with the public demanding more and more. Willie never ducked an opponent or "played it safe." He took on everyone, on their tables and at their locations: in sunny California on Saturday and bleak, wintry Maine on Monday. The record over the years was so great they didn't even bother to keep it—few won even a game from Willie and no one won a tournament.

But Willie Mosconi has not only been the pocket billiards player supreme, he has been its principal salesman and propagandist. The spectacular resurgence of the game of billiards, and particularly pocket billiards, is due in no small measure to Willie's missionary efforts. He has been tireless in improving the "image" of billiards and in this campaign has given countless exhibitions before college students, women's groups, and the like. In his role as a consultant to a large manufacturer, Mosconi suggested the introduction of tangerine, blue, white, and gold cloth to replace the traditional green baize and its unfavorable associations. Mosconi also suggested making the pockets as large as legally allowable.

"Why frustrate the new player?" he asked. "Let him make as many shots as possible, and you create a new fan."

Like so many other billiard champions, Willie is the son of a billiard parlor proprietor. However his father, Joseph, forbade Willie to learn the game and actually locked up the cues and balls at night. Joseph wanted Willie to go into show business as a dancer with two of his uncles. One of the uncles played Willie, then aged six, a game of pool and the boy ran off 15 balls. It seems that he had been practicing billiards late at night, using a broomstick and round potatoes in place of the locked-up cues and balls. Recognizing the inevitable, father Joseph arranged a series of exhibitions for his precocious son, who ran 40 balls in a match against a ten-year-old girl in the National Billiard Academy in Philadelphia, Willie's home town. After a few more exhibitions Willie "retired" from billiards at age seven.

"I was sick of the game," Mosconi recalled. "First my dad was trying to stop me from learning it, then he was trying to ram it down my throat." After graduation from high school, Willie went back to billiards when he found jobs scarce because of the Depression. At nineteen he joined the staff of the manufacturing company and decided to make the cue sport his career. His first assignment was a 112-day tour with Ralph Greenleaf, then world pocket billiards champion. Greenleaf won 57 matches to Mosconi's 50, but most of Willie's wins came near the end of the tour, indicating that he had absorbed much of value from playing and closely observing Greenleaf.

When Mosconi won the 1941 World Championship in a six-month tournament, the *National Bowlers Journal* reported: "Who ever heard of winning a world crown by 32 games? Mosconi did it. The youthful expert from Philly won seven games by 125-and-out, a remarkable feat in any class of pocket competition. Mosconi's performance was nothing short of fantastic. He had 50 runs of 100 or more in his total of 224 games." In the ensuing years Mosconi lost the world title briefly to Jimmy Caras and Irving Crane but regained it. He has not been active in tournaments since suffering a stroke in 1957 but continues with exhibition play and varied publicity work designed to further the cause of billiards.

The annals of billiards competition over the years contain the names of many colorful and compelling champions and near-champions who made lasting contributions to the sport without receiving the acclaim which went to Greenleaf and the two Willies, Hoppe and Mosconi.

It is rare to find a player skilled enough to compete at both straight billiards and the pocket games. A notable exception was the magnificent Spanish cue artist, Alfredo DeOro, a dignified and courtly gentleman who was a member of his country's diplomatic service. DeOro simultaneously competed in both branches of billiards with outstanding success, never duplicated or approached by modern-day practitioners of the game. DeOro won the pocket billiards championship of the world 18 times, beginning in 1887 and extending through 1913. At the same time he won the three-cushion billiards championship of the world 10 times from 1908 through 1919. He began to play in the early age of billiards when equipment was often irregular, yet he took on all challengers at their own game and defeated them. He earned the great respect of opponents and audiences, both as a player and as a person.

Charlie Peterson was a wizard with a cue who could perform an amazing variety of trick shots. "Show me a shot I can't make!" was his famous war cry as he traveled across the country giving exhibitions at country fairs, in school gymnasiums, at church bazaars, and in local billiard emporiums. For 25 years Charlie was the Blackstone, Thurston, and Houdini of the billiard world. (He also held the red-ball carom championship of the world from 1907 through 1944.)

One day in Houston, Charlie went through his repertoire of caroms, banks, billiards, throw shots, combination shots, the machine gun, and the rest and then uttered his famous war cry.

"O.K., stranger, I'll show you a shot you can't make," came the response in a heavy Texas drawl. A big Texan (is there any other kind?) came up to the table, placed two balls close together, and inserted a big silver dollar on edge between them. "Let's see you knock the dollar against the end rail and back between the two balls," the Texan demanded.

"Now there's a trick if I ever saw one," replied Peterson, stalling for time. "How many chances do I get to make the shot?"

"Take three, mister, any three you want," was the reply, as laughter rippled through the room. Charlie muttered something about taking his war cry out of service and took his first try at what looked an impossible shot. The coin sped down the table and rebounded in a crazy arc, missing the two target balls by three feet, but Charlie suddenly realized the shot could be made. On his next try he leveled the cue and reduced the forward thrust; the silver dollar hit the rail and rebounded into one of the balls. On the third try, Charlie sent the coin into the rail and back through the narrow slot. The Texans erupted in a bedlam of acclaim and carted Charlie off to the bar for a celebration drink. Later Charlie added that shot to his bag of tricks. On occasion he managed to make the coin come to a dead stop between the two balls—a trick never equaled by any other trick-shot artist.

No discussion of top billiard players would omit mention of Welker Cochran, whose three-cushion matches with Willie Hoppe during the 1930s were classics of billiard history. Cochran learned the game in his father's billiard parlor in Manson, Iowa, and became the protege of Frank Gotch, the wrestler, who arranged for the lad to study billiards under the fine Chicago teacher, Lanson Perkins. At seventeen Cochran beat everybody but Hoppe in a handicap tournament in New York, which was the start of their celebrated rivalry. Cochran won the 18.2 balk-line billiards title in 1927 and 1934 and later became three-cushion champion six times. He defended the title in 1944 from Hoppe in a dramatic 4,800-point ninety-game match played in 13 cities. Cochran won it by 48 points at the San Francisco Olympic Club.

Cochran was a precise, dedicated individual who trained for a match like a boxer. He used to do regular roadwork around the reservoir in Central Park. One morning, when he had a match coming up with his old rival Hoppe, he met that opponent jogging the other way round the reservoir.

Australia, which is better known as a nursery of top tennis players and swimmers, produced in the late Walter Lindrum a genius of the cue "who could make breaks with a walking stick and three oranges," as one awed writer put it. Lindrum so far outdistanced his opponents on the large English billiards tables that he actually ran out of competitors. The English officials changed the rules of the game to try to even things up for his challengers, but it made no difference. Lindrum murdered them under the new rules. In 1933 he set a world record break of 4,137 at Thurston's, the "home" of English billiards in Leicester Square, London. This staggering performance led officials to pass a rule prohibiting more than 15 consecutive nursery cannons—Lindrum's favorite shot. They also made a new balk-line rule, requiring a player to cross the balk line between each succeeding 180 and 200 points. "It makes no difference." Lundrum shrugged. "I'll play under any rules they like."

Shortly afterward, according to the Sydney *Sunday Telegraph*, Lindrum piled up a break of 2,466 under the new rules and, a few years later, ran a total of 3,361—far ahead of any opponents. Lindrum accepted a challenge from a South African syndicate to play their star, Frank Ferraro, in a fortnight's winner-take-all match for £500, with Lindrum to give his opponent a 5,000-point start. At the last moment the syndicate backed out, and Lindrum offered Ferraro 20,000 points. The South African could not refuse this apparent "gift," the *Telegraph* recalled, and the match was on.

Lindrum was in devastating form and seemed able to score as and when he wished, the Australian newspaper reported. By the end of the first week, Ferraro was hopelessly behind. In order to retain public interest in the match, Lindrum gave his unhappy opponent 7,000 more points, making a total "gift" of 27,000 points. Despite this magnanimous gesture, Lindrum won the match with ease.

The high point of Lindrum's career was not the Ferraro victory but his "command performance" in Buckingham Palace for their late Majesties, King George V and Queen Mary in 1931. This scheduled one-hour exhibition stretched to 3½ hours as the royal couple, both keen billiard players, asked the Australian cue wizard to stay on and give them personal instruction. As Lindrum left, he expressed his thanks and said he felt "like a king." His Majesty smiled, waved his cue, and replied he felt "like a Lindrum."

Having run out of qualified opponents, Lindrum opened a billiard parlor in Melbourne and contented himself with practice matches against his customers. But when World War II broke out he closed the establishment, donated its 50 tables to the troop camps, and went on an extended tour, in which he gave more than 3,000 exhibitions and raised more than one million pounds for charity. When Lindrum finally retired in 1950, he relinquished his world title at English billiards and returned to the English Billiards Association the championship cup which he had held unchallenged for seventeen years.

It is not only the big winners who provide the excitement in billiard competition. George Chenier, the smooth little Canadian champion whose specialty is snooker, the highly demanding English version of pocket billiards, came to New York in 1963 for the world championship pocket billiards round robin to meet 11 other top-flight players. Chenier, who lost four of his first five matches, did not win any of the trophies, but I watched him cause one of the great sensations of modern-day competition as he defeated Irving Crane, an American ex-world champion, and one of the very best players in the world today, by the astonishing score of 150 to 0. It was the first time a run of this length had been scored under the pressure of a world championship. Experts called it the equivalent of pitching a no-hitter in a World Series game against the New York Yankees or of bowling 300 in the American Bowling Congress tournament.

In the practice room before their match, Chenier looked forlorn and tired as he half-heartedly ran a rack of balls. He had yet to win a match in the tournament, while his youthful-appearing, confident opponent had won three times and was the tournament favorite. But the gods of chance had a shock in store for Crane—one which came as even a bigger shock to Chenier. The American won the lag and elected to have the Canadian break. The break was not too good, but Crane then tried a safety play which misfired by leaving Chenier an easy shot with a lone ball near the top center spot. The little Canadian sharpshooter pocketed the ball, made a two-cushion bank, and broke the pack and for the next hour and a half had the balls flying into pockets at his every command as he made a clean sweep of the match. Crane was desolated, but the audience wildly applauded Chenier in his great moment of glory.

As it developed, neither Crane nor Chenier finished "in the money" in the world championship, which was won by Luther Lassiter, the courtly Southern gentleman who defended his title a few months later with success against Cowboy Jimmy Moore in a two-man series at the New York Athletic Club.

Lassiter, a forty-five-year-old bachelor who neither smokes nor drinks anything stronger than soda pop, is a champion who will add gloss to the new image of billiards. His behavior at the table and away from it is impeccable. Fond of quoting the Bible during tight spots in a match, Lassiter is a genial, humorous man without an enemy in the world. Having watched him in every match he played in his recent world title matches, I reached the conclusion that he has everything a great champion must have—skill, poise, artistry, personality, coolness under fire, the ability to win or lose gracefully, plus that saving grace, a sense of humor.

Lassiter hails from Elizabeth City, North Carolina, where he took up billiards at age fourteen, playing with a neighboring physician on a homemade table with only four pockets. A few years later he was getting instruction in Norfolk from the legendary New York Fats, Rudy Wanderone, at the latter's billiard parlor. (Wanderone, a large, outgoing individual, is widely believed to have been the inspiration for the part of Minnesota Fats portrayed by Jackie Gleason in *The Hustlers.*)

Lassiter was unfortunate to come along in billiards when the game was at low ebb, when world competition was virtually nonexistent. He won a world tournament in Philadelphia in 1954 the legality of which was subsequently challenged, but he was not invited to participate in the four-handed tournament which settled the dispute. A serious stomach operation hampered his play for some years, and he still suffers from gall bladder trouble which plagues him during close matches. But Lassiter's courtly manners and gallant sportsmanship never desert him, despite his afflictions. In the New York world championship in

1963, Lassiter suffered only one loss against 11 competitors. When he was beaten by Cowboy Jimmy Moore, Luther laid down his stick, went over to Moore, and shook his hand warmly, drawling, "You sure are a fine player—my congratulations." He obviously meant it.

In the practice session at the Hotel Commodore's grand ballroom before his final match, Lassiter courteously answered questions from spectators as he stroked the balls. "Yes, I travel around quite a bit . . . Yes, I'll gamble now and then. . . . Yes, I just got over a gall bladder operation." With each answer he would knock in a ball. He paused and looked at the table, where he had three shots left, two fairly easy and one difficult. "I can't eat steaks any more," he murmured. *Bang*—in went the first ball. "I can't do any drinking." *Bang*—in went the second ball. "All the things I like to do I can't do." *Bang* went the third shot. The table was cleared, Lassiter took a drink of water, popped a peppermint wafer into his mouth, and walked over to the championship table for his last match.

In the next hour he showed us what he really likes to do and can do as well as anyone in the world—play billiards.

PART TWO

Billiards for Beginners

THE FACTUAL MATERIAL presented in this section has been judiciously selected after close observation of professional players and from knowledge of the needs of the beginning player. Information from books, periodicals, photographs, and other sources has been helpful in working out these principles. Most beneficial of all, however, was the practice time spent at the billiard table in proving or disproving theories. In playing and teaching the game, it is possible to develop ideas which may look good on paper but do not work out on the table.

These instructions in the essential elements of billiards are offered you therefore after years of study and after successful practical application by novices as well as experienced players. We shall deal in facts and figures, in diagrams and mathematical equations, but the human factor in billiards is the most important element of all. What you do or do not do at the table will express, to a degree, what kind of person you are. Billiards will bring out the best and the worst in you and reward or punish you, as the case may be. Your success or failure in billiards is all your own doing; the balls roll only in response to your actions.

At first you will feel lost trying to do a whole series of things at once—and probably not doing any of them very well. But do not let discouragement get you down. Keep practicing and studying the material in this book. In time you will become a better than average player, and the better you become the more you will enjoy the game.

1

Equipment

OVER THE COURSE of the years the specifications and dimensions of the equipment used in billiards have become standardized, so that no matter where you play the game you will be using the same size balls on the same size table and using approximately the same size cue stick.

TABLES

Tables come in various sizes, but they are always twice as long as they are wide. They range from 4 by 8 feet to 5 by 10 feet. Tables used for carom billiards have no pockets. Those used for pocket billiards have six pockets—one at each corner and one midway on each long side. The corner pockets vary in size from 4⅞ inches minimum to 5⅛ inches maximum. The two side pockets are larger, ranging from 5⅜ inches minimum to 5⅝ inches maximum.

The bed of the table is usually made of slate, covered with smooth felt. This was formerly a uniform green in color but now may be any variety of bright colors—gold, beige, or blue. The playing surface of the table is from 30 to 31 inches from the floor and is surrounded by rails 1¾ inches high which are shielded with rubber cushions. Modern tables are made of a variety of woods, plastic materials, and aluminum.

BALLS

Ivory, the traditional material for making billiard balls, has been supplanted in recent years by plastics. Pocket billiard balls are 2¼ inches in diameter and carom billiard balls are slightly larger, 2⅜ inches in diameter. Three balls are required for carom billiards. In pocket billiards a cue ball is used, along with fifteen object balls consecutively numbered.

CUES

Cues may vary in weight from 14 to 22 ounces and are approximately 57 inches long. Cue tips are from 11 to 14 millimeters in width; they are always chalked during play to keep them from slipping off the ball. Selection of the proper cue stick is a personal matter. Proper balance and "feel" are important in choosing the right cue. Many advanced players acquire their own cues, jointed in the middle so they may be disassembled and carried in a special case. Pocket billiard cues run from 16 to 18 ounces, billiard cues from 18 to 22 ounces. Snooker cues weigh between 16 and 18 ounces.

Other essential items of equipment are wooden triangles for racking the balls in pocket billiards and long-handled mechanical bridges to assist in making shots from awkward positions on the table.

2

Billiard Terms

Angle

In a simple carom, *angle* refers to the angle at which the cue ball must leave the first object ball to strike the second object ball; also, when cushion contact is required, the angle the cue ball must travel to the first cushion.

Bank

A *bank* is a rebound from a cushion. A bank shot in pocket billiards means a shot in which the cue ball strikes the object ball, which is banked off a cushion and into a pocket.

Break

In carom and pocket billiards, *break* is the first shot in the game: a player shooting first must break the racked object balls. A *break* in snooker refers to a string of consecutive scoring plays.

Bridge

A *bridge* refers to the placement of the left (or right) hand on the table for the purpose of guiding the cue tip in making a shot. A *bridge* is also an elongated cue with a notched, fanlike tip which is used for making shots that are difficult to reach, or which cannot be made with a hand bridge because of the presence of interfering balls or because of excessive distance for comfortable hand bridge.

Called Ball

A *called ball* is the ball a player announces he intends to pocket, giving the number of the ball and the pocket into which it is to be played.

Carom	*Carom* is the action of deflecting one ball from another or from a ball to a rail or rails. *Carom* is also a term used in scoring.
Cushion	The *cushion* is the sharp-edged cloth-covered, rubber-like rail bordering the table.
Dead Ball	A *dead ball* is one that stops upon contact with another ball.
Draw	A shot in which the cue ball, stroked below center, draws back from the object ball after striking it.
English	Spin imparted to a cue ball by cueing it either to the left or the right of center, or from the top of the ball, as in massé.
Feathering	The contact by the cue ball on the edge of the object ball is often so minute that it is called *feathering*. In general, contact of 3/16, 1/8, 1/16, 1/32, 1/64, etc., are feathered shots.
Follow	A shot in which the cue ball is stroked above the center, producing imperfect rotation, which causes it to follow the object ball after contact with it.
Foot spot	The guide spot on the table for racking balls on pocket billiards and other games.
Frozen	When two object balls, or a cue ball and an object ball, are touching each other on the table, they are said to be *frozen*. (A ball that is resting against the cushion may also be called *frozen*.)
Head spot	Center spot on the table (center of length and width) at second diamond distance from head of table.
Inning	A player's turn at the table is called an *inning*.
Kiss	*Kiss* is a kind of carom. See *The Kiss Shot*, pages 85, 86, 94.

Massé   Imperfect rotation of the cue ball. See *The Massé,* pages 59, 60, 123.

Miscue   When the cue ball is poorly stroked, causing the cue tip to slide off the cue ball, it is called a *miscue.*

Nip stroke   A stroking technique used for many shots that do not require the cue to pass through the cue ball in a forward thrust. It is a jabbing stroke with wrist action: downward for a *draw nip stroke*; level for a *forward nip stroke.*

Piquet   A draw shot which reverses direction without striking an object ball. See page 122.

Rack   The triangular wooden frame used to place balls on the foot spot is called a *rack.* Frequently, *rack* refers to the balls themselves.

Safety   A *safety* is a sacrifice. A player may pass up the chance to score in order to put the cue ball in a difficult spot for his opponent's next play.

Scratch   *Scratch* frequently refers to pocketing the cue ball inadvertently, or miscueing. The penalties for scratching vary with different games.

Spot ball   *Spot ball* may mean a ball placed on the table at the start of a game; also a ball inadvertently pocketed in a game such as rotation.

Three-cushion shot   In three-cushion billiards, a cue ball must strike three cushions before, or after, striking the first object ball. See page 131.

3

Types of Games and General Rules of Play

THERE are two basic types of billiard games: carom billiards, played on a table without pockets, as we have said, and pocket billiards, played on a table with six pockets.

There are innumerable varieties of games played in both categories of billiards, and all have their firm adherents. However, in this book I shall confine my descriptions to the most popular games in carom and pocket billiards.

CAROM BILLIARDS

All carom games are played with three balls, one red and two white; one of the white balls carries a small black dot. The most elemental game requires the player to cause the cue ball to contact the other two balls to score a point, or carom. In general, the object is to keep all three balls as closely together as possible so that caroms can be more easily made. Up to eight can play. One to four players is preferable; two players desirable.

To begin the game the players "lag" for the break. The "lag" is a procedure in which each player propels a ball from the head of the table to the foot of the table and has it return to as near the head end rail as possible. The player who is the closest to the head rail has the option of beginning the game or having his partner do so.

Quite often two players will resort to the simple device of tossing a coin to determine "by chance" the rotation of play; but in championship play the element of chance is omitted and the "lag" made mandatory so that the skill factor is the most important element.

In winning the "lag" the player also wins the choice of which cue ball he desires to use: pure white or white with black spot.

Opening the game. A red ball is spotted on foot spot on table and one white ball is on head spot (center) and the other one within six inches of it to the right or the left. First player must contact red ball first and then the game begins. After that he has choice of which one of the two object balls he desires to hit first. See page 128.

Safety play. The player may elect to play safe by driving an object ball to a cushion or by causing the cue ball to strike a cushion after it contacts an object ball. If he succeeds in making a legal safety play, there is no penalty. He merely loses his inning at the table. If he does not succeed (if, for instance, he strikes an object ball but the cue ball doesn't contact a rail), there is a penalty: loss of one point.

Jumped balls. If a cue ball jumps off the table, it is a foul, with a penalty loss of 1 point. The ball is replaced on the foot spot. If that spot is obstructed by another ball, it is placed on the center spot.

If the red ball jumps the table, it is placed on the foot spot.

If the white object ball jumps the table, it is placed on the head spot.

Push or shove shots. A push shot is one in which the tip of the cue remains in constant contact with the cue ball after the cue ball strikes an object ball or when the cue tip contacts the cue ball the second time.

These shots are generally illegal and result in the loss of point. In championship play the opinion of the referee is final. They are illegal in all carom games, but in pocket billiards a push shot with a continuous follow-through stroke is legal—the referee being the final arbitrator as to its validity.

Cueing the ball. If the player contacts the cue ball during his warm-up stroking, it is a foul, with a penalty loss 1 point—loss of inning at the table.

Miscue. As a general rule, miscues are not fouls. However, an intentional miscue may result in a foul, and in professional play the referee may have to decide whether other balls were rearranged so as to cause an intentional hazard, or whether the side of the cue contacted the cue ball after the tip miscued, or whether improper propulsion was transmitted by the device of using a miscue. (These are very advanced plays and for the beginners the rule of thumb is to merely allow the miscue and have the penalty of loss of inning imposed upon the person who miscued.)

Shooting out of turn. If a player shoots out of turn and makes a score, the infraction must be detected before he scores again. If the foul has been detected, there is a loss of 1 point. The incoming player accepts the balls as they are, and proceeds. However, if a second, third, or more points have been made before the infraction is noticed, the player continues to the end of his run and the points count. But he must not shoot again until other players have gone to the table, and this new rotation of play prevails.

If a player shoots the wrong cue ball, it is a foul, with a loss of 1 point. Incoming player accepts the balls as they are at the moment.

If a player is responsible for interference with another player, it is a foul, with a loss of 1 point.

Frozen cue ball. If the cue ball is frozen to the rail, it may be played against the rail, but that rail does not count on this first contact. If contact is made with the rail a second time, it is legal contact. The same thing applies with succeeding contacts with that rail.

If the cue ball is frozen to an object ball, the player may shoot away from the ball or may have all balls spotted as of the break, or opening, of the game.

Bounce on rail. A cue ball that rides on the rail and returns to the bed of table is in play.

Foot on floor. All shots must be made with one foot touching the floor. The penalty for not obeying this rule is the loss of 1 point and loss of inning at the table.

Official game. The player who scores the required number of points first wins the game, even though the opponent or opponents had one less turn at the table.

Straight Rail Billiards

In order to score caroms, the cue ball must contact both object balls; or contact the first object ball, then contact one or more rails, and then the other ball.

Balk-line Billiards

Balk-line rules developed because the experts at caroms learned how to "gather the balls" and "nurse" them along the rails and into the corners for long, tedious runs of scoring.

In order to restrict caroms, balk lines are drawn on the table, generally either 14 inches or 18 inches from the sides and ends, and anchor squares marked out where the balk lines meet the rails.

In 14.1 balk-line billiards and 18.1 balk-line billiards (the numbers refer to the distance in inches of the balk lines from the rails), only one carom can be made in a balk area or anchor area before the balls are driven out to another area for further scoring. In 14.2 balk-line billiards and in 18.2 balk-line billiards, two caroms are permitted in a balk or another zone before the balls must be driven out.

Cushion Caroms

This game was also devised to make caroms more difficult to score. It is necessary to contact the cushion with the cue ball either before striking an object ball or after striking the first object ball and before contacting the second.

Three-cushion Caroms

This is a still more difficult game, in which the cue ball must contact three or more cushions, in various ways, as well as both object balls, in order to score. Generally—and in professional play always—two players compete. However, three or four can play. This game is for the advanced player, and a special section is reserved at the end of this book for the Diamond system of playing three-cushion billiards.

POCKET BILLIARDS

The pocket versions of billiards have become in recent years by far the most widely played and most publicized of the two basic billiard games. In pocket billiards, 15 numbered object balls are used, in addition to the cue ball. Points are scored by driving the object balls into any of six pockets located at the four corners of the rectangular table and midway along the two long sides. Two, four, six, or eight players may play; two or four are best.

Players "lag" for opening or toss coin.

Each player must call the number of the ball he intends to pocket and he must designate the pocket. If a player pockets the ball which he called and other balls go into pockets, he scores those balls along with the "called" ball.

If a player misses the called ball, he may hit another ball by accident and drive it to a rail or carom from it with the cue ball and then touch a rail. In this event there would be no foul. But if he missed the called ball and did not hit another ball or drive a ball to a rail or not carom from a ball to a rail, a foul would have been committed and he would lose his turn at the table and be charged with the loss of 1 point.

GENERAL PENALTIES:

1) Failure to break properly, penalty of 2 points.
2) Scratching cue ball into pocket, loss of 1 point.
3) Bouncing cue ball from table, loss of 1 point.
4) Shooting while balls are in motion or spinning.
5) Failure to drive object ball to cushion, as in safety play, loss of 1 point.
6) Failure to drive cue ball to cushion after contacting object ball, as in safety play, loss of 1 point.
7) Contacting cue ball with tip of cue or contacting it with side edge of cue, loss of 1 point for each infraction.
8) Touching cue ball or object balls with hands, clothing, cue shaft, butt, or other than tip of cue, loss of 1 point.

Rotation, or Chicago

This is a most enjoyable game for beginners because two, three, four, or more people can play at the same time.

All 15 balls are racked with one at apex of triangle, 2 and 3 on ends, large denominations in center. The object is to pocket the balls in their numerical order, from 1 to 15.

Starting player hits No. 1 ball and spreads the rack. He is allowed any ball or balls that go in. After that he must hit the lowest-numbered ball remaining on table and score it or cause it to score another ball.

The player with the highest added score of all of his pocketed balls wins the game. If partners have been playing, the combined totals of their numbered balls win. Any score of 61 points or over wins, as the total of 1-15 equals 120 points.

General rules and penalties for pocket billiards prevail in this game.

Fifteen Points

This game, somewhat similar to rotation, is better for two players. One point is scored for each combination of pocketed balls adding up to 15. Thus, if you pocket the No. 6 ball first, you must pocket the No. 9 ball next in order to score a point; if you pocket the No. 3 ball, you must then pocket the No. 12 ball to score. Finally, only the No. 15 ball is left on the table; it counts 1 point when pocketed.

The person with the greatest number of combinations of 15 wins the game.

General rules and penalties for pocket billiards also apply to this game.

Eight Ball

In pocket billiards, balls 1 through 7 are in solid colors, with the numbers circled in white; the No. 8 ball is solid black; the balls 9 through 15 have striped bands. In this game for two players, one player uses the solid-colored low numbers as his object balls and the other takes the striped balls. The first player to pocket all his object balls is permitted to shoot at the No. 8 ball; if he pockets it, he wins the game.

Baseball Pocket Billiards

This is a very popular game for home playing although it is not generally played in the larger rooms. Its popularity seems to be directed toward those sportsmen who are baseball fans, and they enjoy the high scores and spectacular plays that prevail. However, the general billiard player is a kind of specialist for his game and he is more interested in the finer aspects of billiard play than he is in some comparison to another sport. While Baseball Billiards offers lots of fun, it loses an element of skill because lucky shots predominate. This factor does not deter those novices who enjoy baseball on the diamond, on the television, in the newspaper, and in the sports books. If Baseball Billiards is their game, I encourage their participation in it and wish them the greatest pleasure.

There are 21 object balls, numbered 1 through 21, in this game. They are racked in a triangle at the foot spot, which is called "home plate." The No. 9 ball is called "the pitcher." The game is played with from two to nine players, and each player is given nine "innings" in which to score. The one with the most "runs" wins the game. The runs, of course, correspond to the number of the pocketed balls. Scores are posted inning by inning, as in baseball.

Golf Pocket Billiards

This game is played with a single object ball assigned to each player. The object of the game is to play "six holes" in the fewest number of strokes. The object ball must be pocketed in each of the six pockets in rotation and be spotted after each hole (pocket). Two players are desirable for this game, although four can play as two two-man teams.

14.1 Continuous

This is the championship game of pocket billiards, for two players only, usually played on a 4½- by 9-foot table. The object is to make a continuous run of 14 balls, leaving the fifteenth ball on the table. The 14 pocketed balls are then racked again. The player seeks to pocket the fifteenth ball and break the racked balls so as to continue the run. In championship play, the first player to score 150 points wins. Players "call" both ball and pocket in advance and receive one point for every ball pocketed.

The skill necessary to pocket 14 balls without error is equal to the mastery demanded of the three-cushion and balk-line billiards experts. Both types of billiard games require a high sense of generalship, complete command of position play, knowledge of all aspects of billiards, and nerves of steel. Each type has its own special pitfalls and rewards, and there are few players who are equally proficient at all games of billiards.

AMERICAN SNOOKER

Twenty-one object balls (15 red, 6 colored) and a white cue ball are used in this game. The table may vary in size: 5 by 10 feet or 6 by 12 feet, or even 4 by 8 feet or 4½ by 9 feet. The height of the table should be from 31 to 32 inches to the top of the rail cap. There should be six pockets, the corner ones from 3⅜ inches to 3⅝ inches; the side ones either 4-1/16 or 4-5/16 inches.

Each ball has a designated spot for its number and color.

The players "lag" or draw lots for opening the game. The player who starts it must pocket a red ball (thereby winning 1 point) before he can continue. He must then select a colored numbered ball, announce his choice, and proceed to pocket it. (He does not have to announce which pocket he intends to use.) If he makes his shot, he adds the number on the ball to his score.

The player continues to pocket balls, alternating red ones (which he does not have to call) with colored ones (which he must call). When all the red balls are off the table, the remaining colored ones must be taken in numerical order.

Red balls, once pocketed, are never spotted, even if they are thrown into a pocket by another ball. Colored balls are spotted on their original spots after being pocketed *if* there are red balls on the table. If an original spot is occupied, the ball is spotted on the next-lower number.

In scoring, red balls count 1 point; colored balls have the value of the numbers on them. If the cue ball jumps the table, there is a 1-point loss. If a numbered ball jumps the table, it is spotted on its original location. Fouling players cannot score on a fouling stroke.

A player is said to be "snookered" if he cannot shoot in a straight line at a ball because there are other balls in the way. If he is snookered on the red balls, he must still try to hit one of them without hitting a numbered ball first, and if necessary must make a bank shot in order to do so. Contact with the numbered ball first means a foul. The same thing applies, in reverse, to being snookered on the colored balls.

4

Bridges

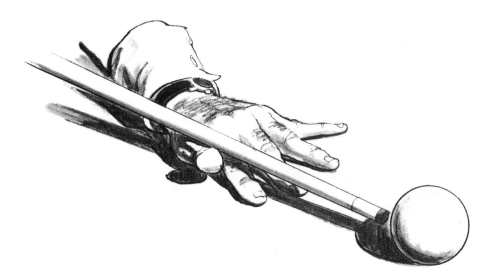

1.   This is the easiest bridge to make and one often used by women and children. To form the bridge, place the hand flat on the table, thumb touching first finger, and spread out the other fingers to obtain firm support. For the vast majority of shots, the cue should be held as nearly parallel to the surface of the table as possible.

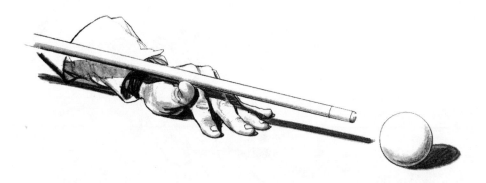

2. To control the elevation of the cue, the fingers are extended outward or drawn in toward the palm of the hand. Here the fingers are drawn in, raising the cue so as to strike the ball high, for a follow shot.

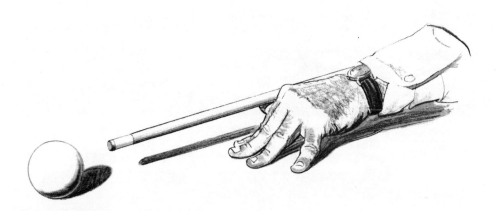

3. Here the base of the hand is raised off the table in order to keep the wrist and forearm clear of other balls.

4. This fingertip bridge is used to shoot over a ball immediately behind the cue ball. Note how the fingers are spread apart to provide maximum support.

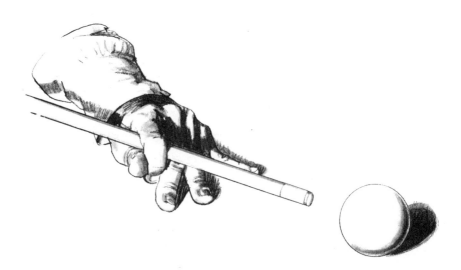

5. This is the standard bridge, used for 80 to 90 per cent of all shots. Its principal advantages are security and adaptability.

Note that the base of the hand is on the table and the fingers are spread for support; the first finger is looped over the cue shaft; the thumb is pressed against the first finger firmly but not too tightly, controlling pressure on the shaft. The standard bridge produces a kind of straight-edge or ruler effect, since the cue shaft touches the fingers at two points: the base of the thumb and near the middle joint of the middle finger. This is an important advantage, for it enables the player to control the forward thrust of the cue in the desired straight line with two contact points on the fingers. The cue often veers off line with only one contact point.

6. To make a draw shot, the fingers are extended, lowering the cue so that the ball will be struck low, thus imparting backspin.

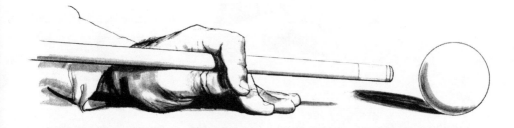

7. This is the standard bridge for people with short fingers. Merely place thumb on edge of middle finger and then overlap first finger.

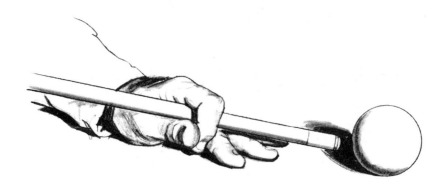

8.   This bridge is for a standard draw shot. Note the base of hand on table; fingers spread for firmness, with thumb and first finger holding cue shaft firmly. The distance from the bridge to the cue ball is between 6 and 8 inches. The cue stick is held as nearly parallel to the table as possible.

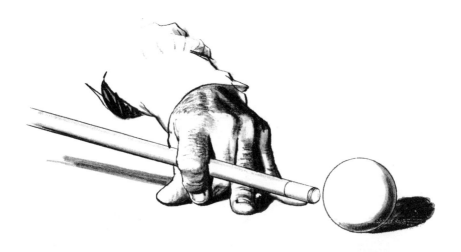

9.   This bridge is a variation of the one for a standard draw shot. Note that the middle finger is turned in and resting on the table. This provides excellent support when necessary to raise the butt end of the cue to avoid contacting balls in the area.

10. For the nip draw shot, place knuckles on table and shorten the distance from the cue ball to between 4 and 6 inches. The shot is a quick jab into the cue ball and the results are frequently excellent. This shot is possible whenever the cue ball is close to the object ball.

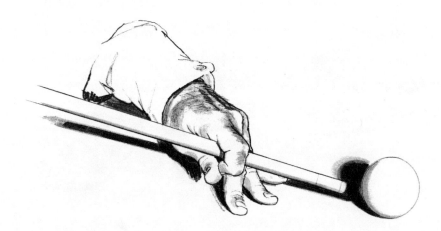

11. This bridge is for a shot made with the base of the hand raised off the table. It is used for piquet and jump shots, generally for exhibition purposes.

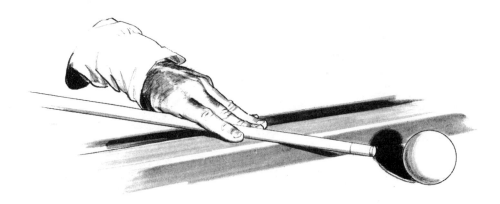

12. This is a rail bridge. Note the straight-edge effect of the thumb on the inside of the cue shaft and the edge of the middle finger. The first finger holds the cue shaft firmly against these two points. The cue rides on the rail edge of the table.

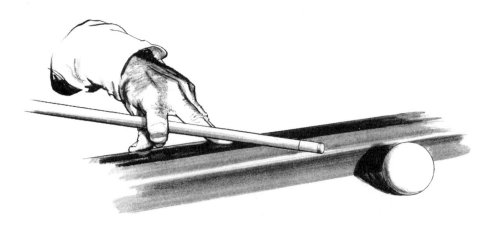

13. Here is another type of rail bridge. Note the thumb pressing against the rail edge, giving security and firmness to the bridge. Inside of thumb and inner edge of middle finger are the two points of the straight edge.

14. This diagram shows the use of a mechanical bridge. This aid is held firmly on the base of the table, on an angle to the cue ball. The shot is made with the elbow elevated.

15. Here is a double mechanical bridge, designed to attain extra height when shooting over a ball behind the cue ball.

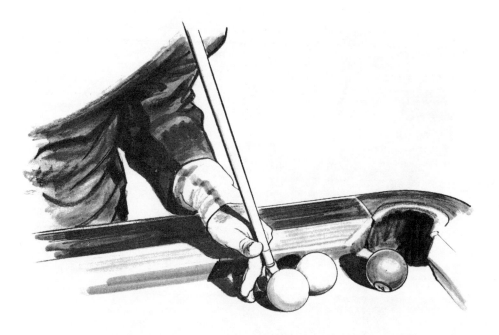

16. This bridge is used for a massé executed with the cue elevated and a downward thrust.

17. This bridge is used for a massé executed with both hands off the table. The left arm is held tightly against the body; the right hand remains flexible and imparts a snappy wrist action to the cue ball.

18. This is a standard bridge shot, showing the fingers spread for stability and the cue in line with the eyes and the right arm.

19. For proper grip, hold the cue firmly but lightly between the thumb and fingers of the right hand.

20. This shows the proper position to execute the jump shot. The cue ball jumps over the first two object balls and drives the third object ball into the side pocket.

21. Here is a standard break shot.

5

English

EVERY competent book on billiards, and every expert of the game, has stressed the technique of center ball play before going on to the use of spin or English on the cue ball. We are no exception to this rule. We advise the beginner to have the same sort of respect for the mechanics of billiards that he would have for the power in a sports car.

Let us look at different ways to use English. The A B C's of English are basic for all games of billiards, so you might just as well learn them right now. Remember, you are learning how to play, and learning slowly and thoroughly. Do not rush through the alphabet. There is pleasure in every step of the way.

When you have mastered one phase of the game, new horizons will open to you and new challenges will command your attention.

POINTS TO REMEMBER

THE FIRST THING a beginner must master, after he learns how to stroke the cue ball, is a working knowledge of the angles the cue ball takes off an object ball. This is vital for playing carom billiards and is important for positioning the cue ball in pocket billiards.

The beginner uses angles in a haphazard way, bouncing one ball off another and trusting to luck or chance for results. Here are a few pointers which will help you make the proper angles with intelligence and skill.

1. In learning the technique of making proper angles, use center ball stroking on the cue ball, at the beginning.

2. With center ball stroking, use mild pressure on the cue ball at first.

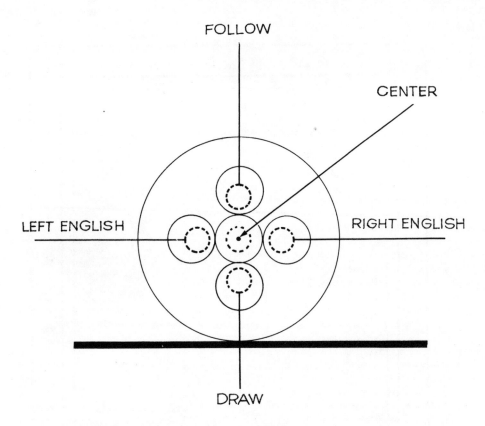

FOLLOW

CENTER

LEFT ENGLISH

RIGHT ENGLISH

DRAW

FRONT VIEW OF CUE BALL SHOWING AIM POINTS

3. Keep the cue level and keep your eye on the spot on the object ball you intend to hit.

4. Observe carefully the action of the cue ball as it caroms off the object ball.

5. In practicing, gradually increase the distance between the cue ball and the object ball.

6. Try using top English on the cue ball (see the diagrams on pages 66, 68); practice first with top left English, then top right English.

7. Now use low English on the cue ball; practice first with low left English, then low right English. Use soft pressure, at first; then increase the amount of force on the cue ball and observe the results.

8. In making draw shots, using low English, better results are obtained if the bridge hand is close to the cue ball and the hand is securely placed on the table.

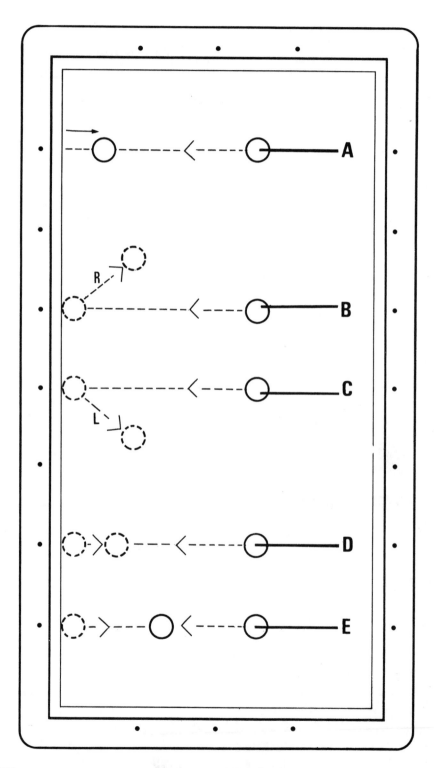

FRONT VIEW **SIDE VIEW**

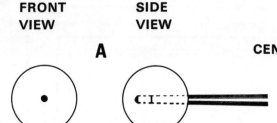

A

CENTER BALL

Level cue. Stroke through the cue ball. Ball rebounds in direct line with point of aim.

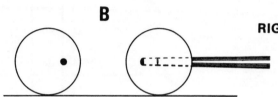

B

RIGHT SIDE SPIN

Level cue. Stroke through cue ball. Rebounds to right.

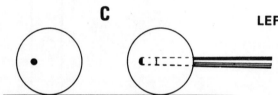

C

LEFT SIDE SPIN

Level cue. Stroke through cue ball. Rebounds from cushion to left.

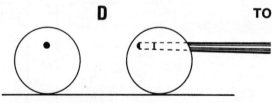

D

TOP FOLLOW

Level cue. Stroke through cue ball. Rebounds from cushion in direct line of aim.

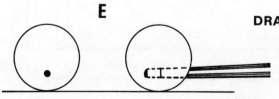

E

DRAW SHOT

Cue very slightly inclined. Snappy wrist and smart follow through. Ball returns in direct line of aim.

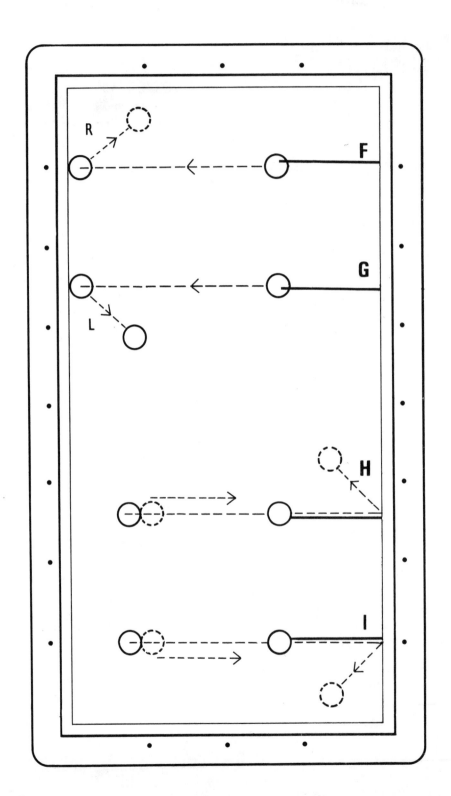

F

DRAW OFF RAIL

Right English. Slightly inclined cue. Smooth snappy stroke.

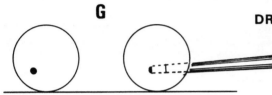

G

DRAW OFF RAIL

Left English. Slightly inclined cue.

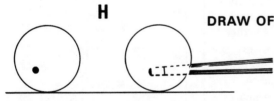

H

DRAW OFF OBJECT BALL TO RAIL

Left English produces right direction of cue ball rebound off rail.

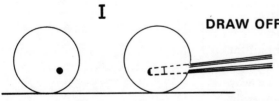

I

DRAW OFF OBJECT BALL TO RAIL

Right English produces left direction of cue ball rebound off rail.

6

Eighteen Practice Lessons
for All Games of Billiards

ONE: CENTER STROKE

The objective is to hit the ball with center stroke, so that it travels to the foot of the table and rebounds in a direct line, passing over the head spot where it started.

How to do it: Place a single ball on the table midway between the side rails, on the head spot. Step back from the table and walk up to the ball facing forward. Place your left hand (or right, for left-handed players) on the table and make the proper bridge. Turn your body 45 degrees to the right (or left) and check your stance, so that your body weight is evenly balanced and you feel comfortable.

Keep your head over the cue shaft in the line of aim.

Hold the cue lightly in your right hand. Aim through the center of the ball to the spot on the rail at the foot of the table. Deliver a center ball hit with a smooth thrust, using enough power to propel the ball all the way to the foot of the table and back again to the head rail.

Do not be discouraged if the ball does not pass over the starting spot. This is not an easy shot to make, particularly for beginners. But it is a basic stroke for the game of billiards.

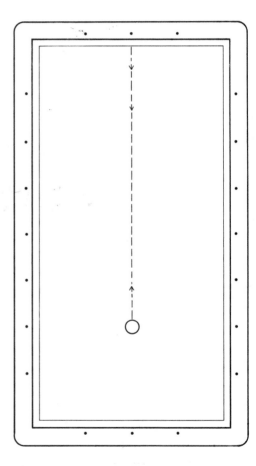

Practice this stroke until you are reasonably proficient, and the other lessons will come easier.

TWO: ENGLISH

The objective is to learn the effect of English, or spin, on the cue ball.

How to do it: Place a single ball on the table at the head spot, as in Lesson One. First hit the cue ball slightly right of center on its horizontal axis and aim directly at the center of the rail at the foot of the table. Stroke the ball with your cue held level, and follow through after you hit the ball. Note that the cue ball rebounds off the rail to the right.

Now hit the cue ball slightly left of center on its horizontal axis, also aiming directly at the center spot on the foot of the table. Note that the cue ball rebounds off the rail to the left.

This illustrates in simple fashion the effect of imparting English to the cue ball. Practice hitting the ball at various speeds and at various distances from the foot rail and observe the varying reactions of the ball.

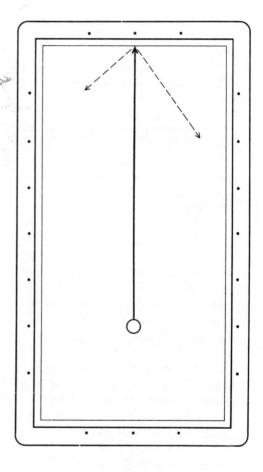

THREE: HITTING THE OBJECT BALL

The objective is to drive the object ball to the foot rail and hit it in the center.

How to do it: Place the cue ball on the head spot, as in the previous lessons, and place an object ball on the center spot of the table. Chalk your cue tip to avoid miscueing. Step into the shot, taking your proper stance at the table. Keep your eye on the object ball as you try practice swings with your right arm six to twelve inches away from your body, the upper part of the arm held rather rigid and the lower arm and wrist swinging freely.

Look at the target spot in the center of the foot rail. Then aim your cue tip at the center of the cue ball and stroke smoothly, eyes focused on the object ball just before stroking cue ball, and following through after cue meets ball.

Again, this shot is not so easy as it looks, but it can be mastered with practice. First, practice hitting the cue ball in the exact center; then try hitting it above center to observe the follow, or forward movement, of the cue ball; and finally, practice hitting it below the center line, to observe the reverse, or draw, action of the cue ball.

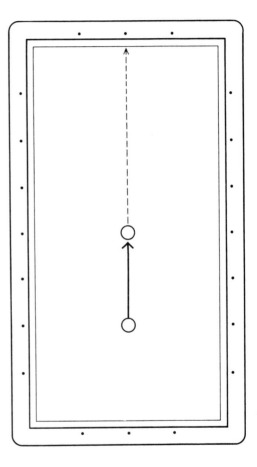

FOUR: SIMPLE CAROMS

The objective is to hit both object balls with the cue ball.

How to do it: The carom action is the bouncing off of one ball by another. Use three balls on the table; the cue ball, one red object ball, and a white object ball. Draw an imaginary line between the centers of object ball 1 and object ball 2. Note the imaginary spot on the far side of object ball 1. Aim the center of the cue ball at this spot. The actual contact point is somewhat to the left of the point of aim, as shown in the illustration. The curvature of the balls is the reason for this seeming disparity.

In making this shot use a high center ball stroke on the cue ball and hold the cue level.

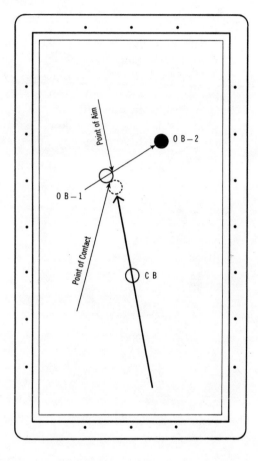

FIVE: USE OF THE FOLLOW BALL
(Carom Billiards)

The objective is to hit both balls with the cue ball.

How to do it: Use the same principle as in Lesson Four. Aim for the spot on the farther side of the first object ball. Place high follow English on the cue ball and employ a smooth stroke.

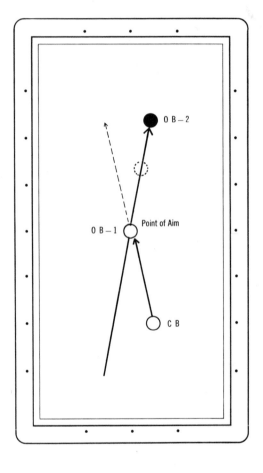

SIX: TARGET SPOTS ON RAIL

(Carom Billiards)

The objective is to hit target spots on the rail with the cue ball.

How to do it: Review Lesson Four. Place an object ball on the table and practice hitting it with the cue ball, with a definite target on the rail. By selecting a point opposite a diamond you can easily find a rail target. This exercise will give you a good "sense of angles."

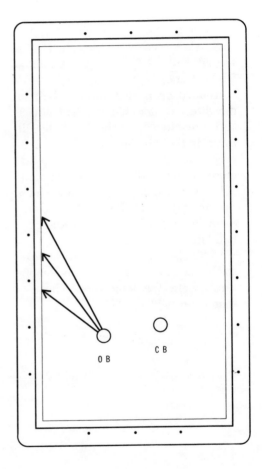

O B

C B

SEVEN: USE OF THE DRAW BALL

(Carom Billiards)

The objective is to make a right-angle shot from one object ball to a second ball, at both a short and a long distance.

How to do it: Hit the cue ball in the direct center. Hit the first object ball four-fifths full. The cue ball will travel in the direction of object ball 2, even when it is placed in the second, more distant, position in the diagram.

Use some right of center English on the cue ball if the shot does not come easily with perfect center-of-the-cue-ball hit.

Hold the cue lightly and stroke softly on the short shot and more firmly with the long shot. The cue should be held level.

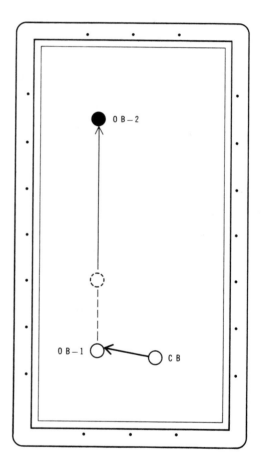

EIGHT: USE OF THE DRAW SHOT

(Carom Billiards)

The objective is to hit two object balls with reverse English, or draw, on the cue ball.

How to do it: Bisect the angle made by drawing a line from the cue ball to the center of the first object ball, and from the second object ball to the center of the first object ball. Note the spot of the bisecting line on the front edge of the first object ball— this is the point of aim for the cue ball. Use a 4-to 6-inch bridge and a snappy draw stroke.

Aim center of cue ball at this spot (point of aim). Actual contact of cue ball will be slightly to right of this, but do not consider that at the time. Concentrate on aiming center of cue ball at point of aim.

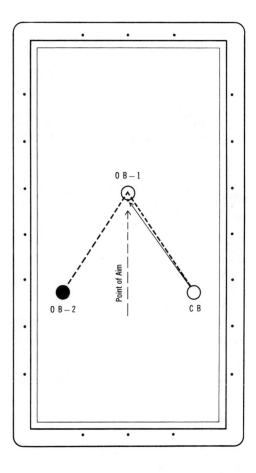

OB–1

Point of Aim

OB–2

CB

NINE:USE OF THE ONE RAIL BANK
WHEN OBJECT BALLS ARE PARALLEL
(Carom Billiards)

The objective is for the cue ball to hit the first object ball, hit the rail, and then strike the second object ball.

How to do it: When the object balls are parallel, draw imaginary lines from both balls to the rail. Bisect the section of the rail between these two lines. The cue ball must strike this mid-point on the rail after hitting the first object ball. Make the shot with follow English and a smooth stroke.

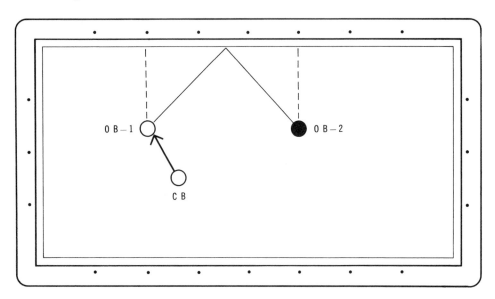

TEN: USE OF THE ONE RAIL BANK
WHEN OBJECT BALLS ARE NOT PARALLEL
(Carom Billiards)

The objective is for the cue ball to hit the first object ball, hit the rail, and then strike the second object ball.

How to do it: When the balls are not parallel to each other, draw imaginary lines from both balls to the rail, as in Lesson Nine. In addition, draw lines from each ball to the spot on the rail measured from the opposite ball (points X and Y) and determine their bisecting point. Draw a line from this bisecting point to the rail. This spot on the rail (Z) is where the cue ball must strike following the carom off the first object ball, so that its rebound path will be in direction of object ball 2.

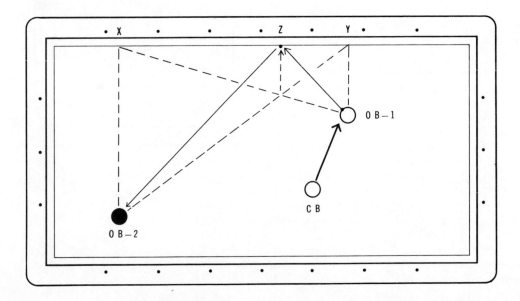

ELEVEN: POCKETING OBJECT BALL

(Pocket Billiards)

The objective is to pocket the object ball in direct line with the pocket.

How to do it: Hit the cue ball in the center with a level cue. Aim at the center spot in line with the pocket. Learn the center ball first, then the follow and draw shots.

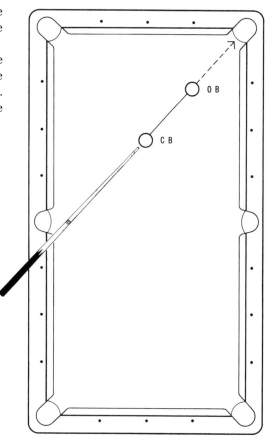

TWELVE: A THROW SHOT

(Pocket Billiards)

The object is to throw the ball into the pocket when it is not in direct line with cue ball and pocket.

How to do it: Use right-of-center English on the cue ball to throw the object ball to the left and into the pocket.

Contact without English would propel the ball to side rail.

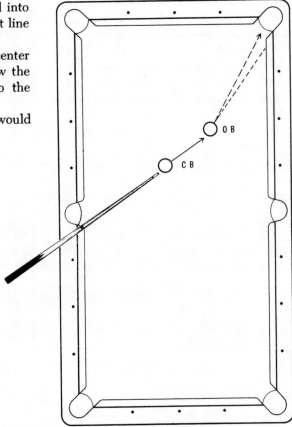

THIRTEEN: ANGLE FOR POCKETING OBJECT BALL
(Pocket Billiards)

The objective is to select the proper angle and put the object ball into the pocket.

How to do it: Draw an imaginary line through the center of the object ball in the direction of the pocket. Aim the cue ball at this spot, but make allowance for the curvature of the outer edges so that the contact points of the cue ball and the object ball meet.

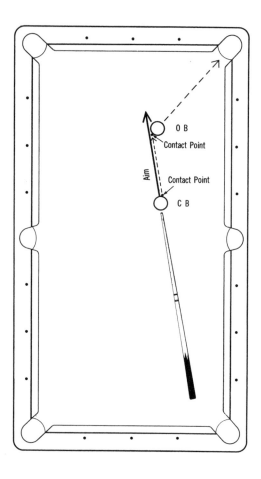

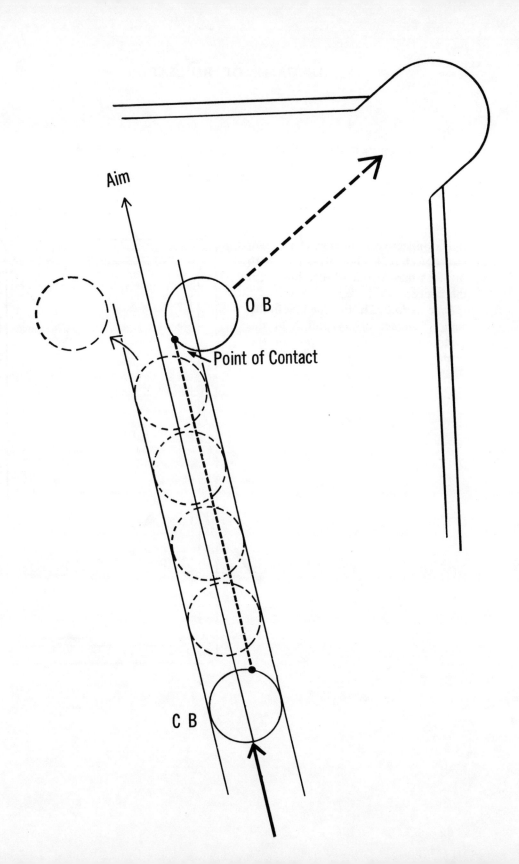

Aim

O B

Point of Contact

C B

FOURTEEN: POCKETING A FROZEN OBJECT BALL
(Pocket Billiards)

The objective is to pocket the second object ball when it is frozen to the first one and in direct line with the pocket.

How to do it: Hit the cue ball in the center; contact object ball 1 in the center; object ball 2 travels to the center of the pocket.

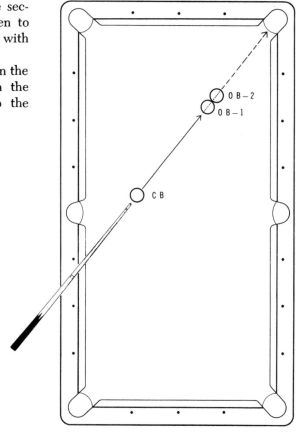

FIFTEEN: A KISS SHOT
WHEN TWO OBJECT BALLS ARE FROZEN
(Pocket Billiards)

The objective is to mesh or kiss the first ball into a pocket when two object balls are frozen.

"Mesh" refers to the effect that the cue ball has in striking the frozen object balls. A player may gauge the effect of this meshing action so that he is able to predict the direction either object ball is going to take.

How to do it: Object balls 1 and 2 are frozen. The line formed by their inner edges is in direct line to the pocket.

If the cue ball strikes object ball 1 on its right side, object ball 1 will take the path of the line to the pocket as it squeezes off of object ball 2.

Use a soft center hit on the cue ball.

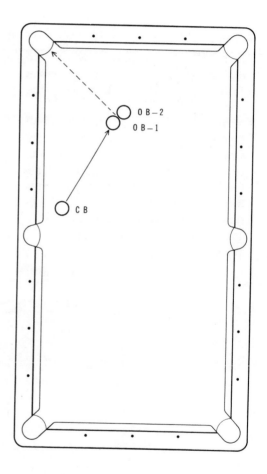

SIXTEEN: A KISS SHOT
WHEN TWO FROZEN OBJECT BALLS
ARE NOT IN LINE WITH POCKET

The objective is to mesh or kiss the first ball into a pocket when two object balls are frozen, as in Lesson Fifteen, but not in line with the pocket.

How to do it: Hit the cue ball below center with drawing action. Contact object ball 1 nearer to the center than in the standard kiss. This forcing shot moves both object balls forward, shifting their line of direction (dotted balls), and object ball 1 takes the proper path toward the pocket.

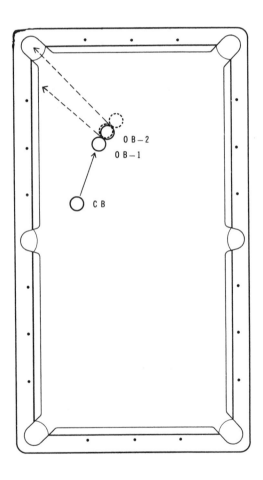

SEVENTEEN: BANK SHOTS WITHOUT ENGLISH

(Pocket Billiards)

The objective is to make bank shots, without English.

How to do it: Draw an imaginary line from the object ball to point *X* on the (far) rail. Draw an imaginary line from the object ball to pocket, also on far side of table. Now draw another imaginary line from X to pocket Y' on near side of table. From the point where these lines intersect, draw a line to the rail Z.

Aim the object ball to hit point Z.

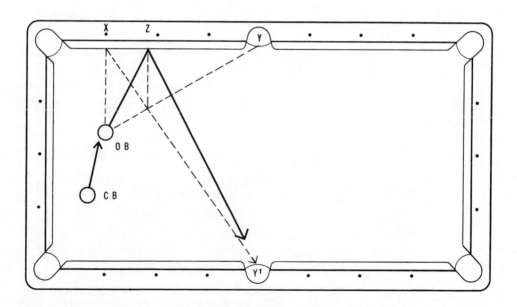

EIGHTEEN: BANK SHOTS, USING ENGLISH

The objective is to make bank shots using English, for those occasions when a ball obstructs the path of the cue ball or the path of the object ball in what would be the natural angle for that particular shot.

How to do it: In order to alter that angle it is possible to use English on the cue ball to affect the action of the object ball as it comes off the rail. Running English on one side of the cue ball will open the natural angle of the object ball, and "reverse English" will close this angle.

Note examples A and B in the illustration and the two different positions on the rail where the object ball strikes it in each example. By using various amounts of English and various speeds of stroke on the cue ball, the opening and closing of the natural angle of the object ball can be changed and controlled.

In A, use left English on the cue ball to drift the object ball to the right and open the natural angle. Right English on the cue ball closes the angle.

In B, use right English on the cue ball to drift the object ball to the left and open natural angle. Left English on the cue ball closes the angle.

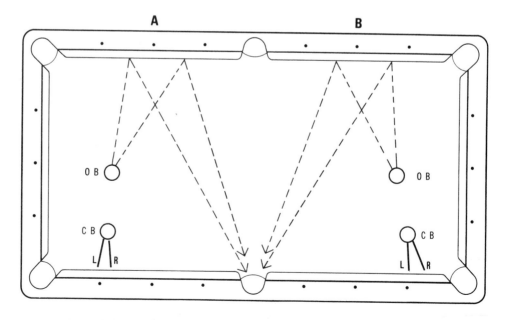

PART THREE

Advanced Shots

THE VARIOUS POINTS of contact between the cue tip and the cue ball in making a shot determine the action the ball takes: normal rotation, abnormal rotation, skidding, massé, and piquet.

As the angle of the cue is varied, the action of the cue ball produces different effects. Moreover, the speed of the stroke, the use of English, and the crispness of execution are all important factors in advanced billiard stroking.

As we have seen, English not only affects the course and impact of the cue ball upon another ball, or cushion: it also affects the action of the object ball after impact and, similarly, the action of the object ball after it has struck the cushion. This is where the game of billiards becomes truly complex.

In this section we shall deal with some of these effects.

1

Carom and Kiss Shots

THE CAROM

The carom action is a major part of billiards, and there is one entire game devoted to carom billiards. Actually, by the use of English, the cue ball, deflecting from an object ball, can cover any spot within a circle (Fig. 1).

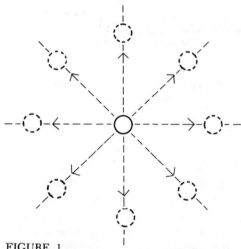

FIGURE 1

In three-cushion billiards, it is necessary to know the carom because in the great majority of shots you must carom from the first object ball in a particular direction into the rail. In Figure 2, the cue ball caroms off object ball 1 to point A on the side rail, to the top rail, to the side rail, to object ball 2 and a score.

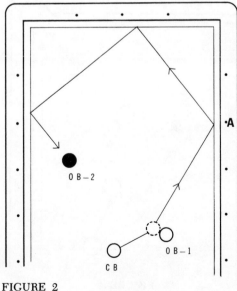

FIGURE 2

In English billiards, you may play a carom off an object ball and "pot" the cue ball for a score (Fig. 3).

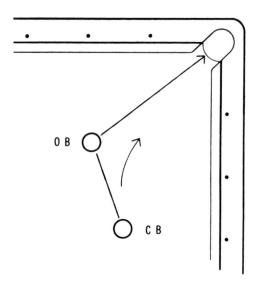

FIGURE 3

In pocket billiards, you may drive an object ball with a second object ball and carom it into a pocket (Fig. 4); or carom from second object ball into any number of other object balls and then into the pocket (Fig. 5).

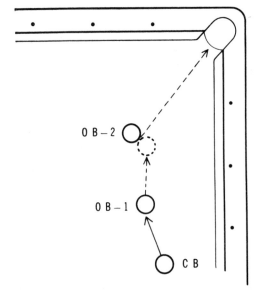

FIGURE 4

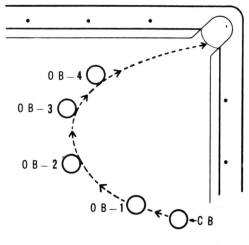

FIGURE 5

How do you determine where to hit the first object ball so as to get the desired direction?

Aim the cue ball at the spot on the far side of a line passing through the center of the object ball to the pocket, as in Figure 6. Actual contact will be to the left of this, but you aim through the object ball at the spot. No English.

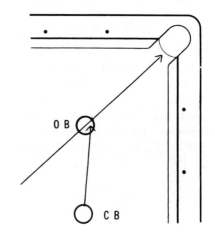

FIGURE 6

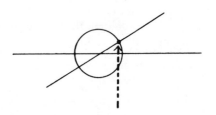

FIGURE 6A

Practice the carom shot so that you build up a kind of storehouse of knowledge. Note the rebound or elasticity of the balls at various points of contact: full ball, three-quarter ball, half ball, one-fourth ball, and a feathering carom. Note the effect of both right and left English on the cue ball, and the effects of follow ball, center ball, draw, and forcing draw on the various points of contact.

Since the amount of pressure which you put into the forward speed of the cue ball has a decided effect upon the action and direction of the cue ball (and the object ball), note these actions and reactions.

THE KISS SHOT

When two balls are frozen, the direction of the first ball is generally in a line which is drawn through the point where the two balls meet. In this case, a moderate center ball hit and no English has the best chance (Fig. 7).

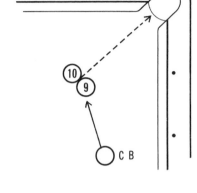

FIGURE 7

By hitting the cue ball low and with force, you may push all balls forward and thus change the direction of the object ball, as in Figure 8.

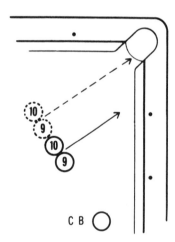

FIGURE 8

In Figure 7, balls 9 and 10 are frozen, and center line is in the direction of the pocket.

Hit ball 9 slightly off center with the cue ball. It will take the direction of the dotted path to the pocket. Use a center-ball or high-ball hit on the cue ball, with a soft stroke, or moderate speed, as desired.

In Figure 8, balls 9 and 10 are frozen, with hit aiming at the side rail. Hit the cue ball low and with strong force, thus forcing balls 9 and 10 forward into the new path direction toward the pocket.

2

Throw Shots

When two balls are frozen as in Figure 9:

A cue ball at (1) hits first ball *a* on left side and throws second ball *b* to the right, away from the pocket, and into the right end rail X.

A cue ball at (2) hits first ball *a* in center as it is lined up with the pocket and throws second ball *b* into the pocket.

A cue ball at (3) hits first ball *a* on right side and throws second ball *b* to left, away from the pocket, and into the left rail Y.

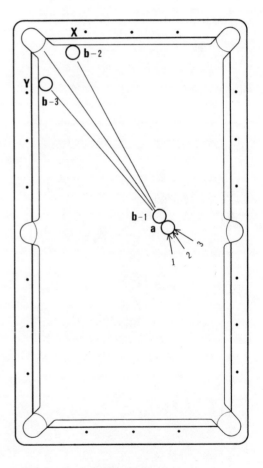

FIGURE 9

Using this throw knowledge, in Figure 10, when balls *a* and *b* are frozen and directed to the end rail, out of the pocket, hit ball *a* with cue tip on the right side and throw second ball *b* into pocket.

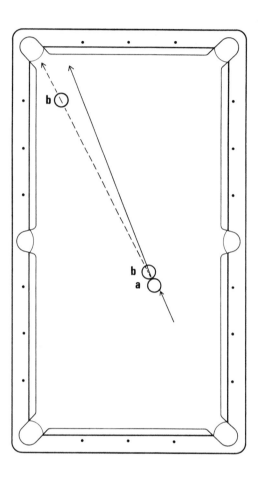

FIGURE 10

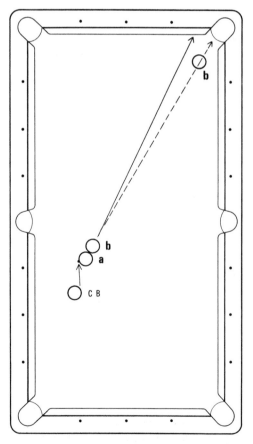

In Figure 11, balls *a* and *b* are frozen but directed toward end rail away from pocket. Hit ball *a* on left side and throw second ball *b* into pocket.

If a third ball (Fig. 12) contacts *a* which is frozen to *b*, it will act as the cue ball did when hitting *a*. The throw will work as in Figures 9, 10, and 11.

FIGURE 11

The third ball, c in this illustration, will contact ball a on the left side and throw ball b to the right and into the pocket. The presence of ball d or any number of additional balls will not change the throw; merely use more force on the cue ball so as to move more balls.

In this case, if ball c were on the right side so as to hit a on the right side, it would throw ball b to the left.

The principle of the a and b frozen balls is that the cue ball will drive ball b in a direct line when it contacts a in the center and will drive ball b in the opposite direction to the side on which ball a is contacted. Thus, if the cue ball hits ball a on the left, it throws ball b to the right; if it hits ball a on the right, it throws ball b to the left.

The third ball, c, may be frozen or not, and it will affect the throw. Fourth, fifth, sixth, seventh, or more balls do not change the action caused by ball c; this is the important ball to observe.

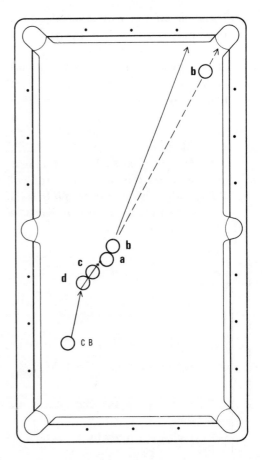

FIGURE 12

VARIOUS DISTANCES

OF THROW

The distance of the balls from the pocket, the angle on the first ball, and the speed on the cue ball all affect the amount of throw.

Thus, when two balls are frozen and headed down the table, and first ball a is hit with a mild amount of pressure by the cue ball, the second ball b will throw a distance off the line of aim by as much as 8 to 12 inches.

By setting up some of these shots in your practice sessions, and hitting a on various points of the horizontal axis left and right of center and with varying amounts of speed on the cue ball, you will build up a knowledge of how much ball *b* will throw under different conditions.

The action in balls *a* and *b* is a kind of meshing action in which the two balls receive energy and direction from the impact of the cue ball. This energy is transmitted in a direct line if the three balls are in a direct line, but when the cue ball hits the first ball off center the energy passes from it into ball *a* and in turn into *b* in such a way (at an angle) as to cause a median change of direction due to the off-center hit.

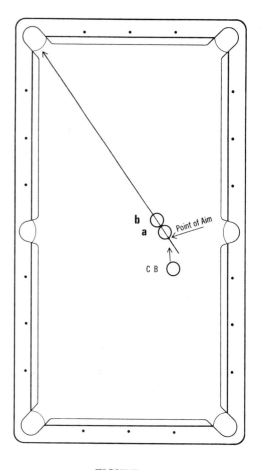

FIGURE 13

CONTACT POINT
AND POINT OF AIM

It is necessary for the player to understand the principle of the contact point and the point of aim.

Because of the curvature of the balls, the side of the object ball nearest you and the farther side of the cue ball do not contact as you might suspect by sighting through the center of the cue ball and aiming at a point on one side or the other of the first object ball.

A line drawn from the center of the pocket through the center of ball *b* and continuing in a straight line indicates the spot on ball *a* to contact with the cue ball. This is called the point of aim (Fig. 13).

In Figure 14, the balls are drawn slightly larger than usual to illustrate the contact point and the point of aim. Generally, in lining up a shot and looking at it from down the table through the cue ball and into the object ball, the front curvature of the object ball and the forward curvature of the cue ball are overlooked, and the player shoots by aiming through the center of the cue ball at a desired spot on the object ball. *This* (14A) *is incorrect.*

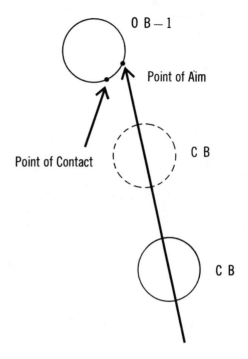

FIGURE 14A

Instead, consider the point of aim and aim the contact point at the point of aim, as in 14B. This will give satisfactory results.

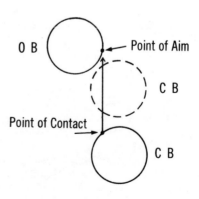

FIGURE 14B

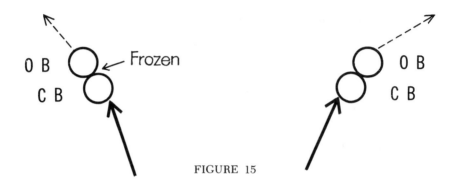

FIGURE 15

Throw shots may be accomplished by the cue ball and one object ball when they are frozen. By merely hitting the cue ball off center, left or right, you can throw the object ball in the opposite direction (Fig. 15). Hold cue level and shoot straight ahead.

Note in Figure 16 that the cue will get the same results at *various angles* of attack into the cue ball. A slightly elevated cue is generally best here, as you wish to stop the forward thrust of the cue ball and yet get throw action on the object ball.

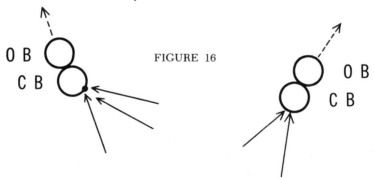

FIGURE 16

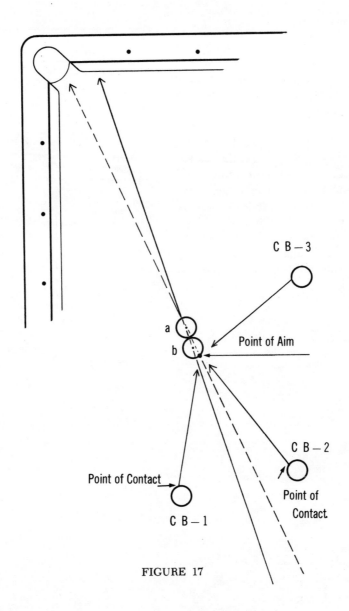

FIGURE 17

The first object ball (*b*) will throw the second object ball (*a*) when the cue ball contacts *b* at a particular spot (point of aim), even if the force from the cue ball comes from various directions, so long as it strikes at that contact point.

Here is an illustration of this point: a single "easy" shot compared with a "harder" combination throw shot. The diagrams are quite similar to point up the comparison.

Figure 18, because of the target area, is really not an easy shot at all; the area of aim and the contact point must coincide or meet in a very small spot. At this distance, it is not so easy to pocket the ball as it may appear. Contact on the object ball must be within a very small area (about ⅛ inch, in this instance, on a regular-size ball).

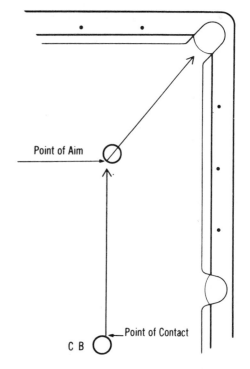

FIGURE 18

The combination throw shot, on the other hand, provides sighting advantages, a wider target area, an opportunity to prevent the cue ball from becoming entangled in other balls—and the cue ball opens the rack of balls.

In Figure 19A, the cue ball contacts *a* on the left side so as to throw *b* into the pocket. This area is about ¼ to ½ inch on a ball, considerably larger than the pinpoint target area in Figure 18.

The cue ball is sighted on the throw area which will give you the throw results. Thus you have a larger area-of-aim.

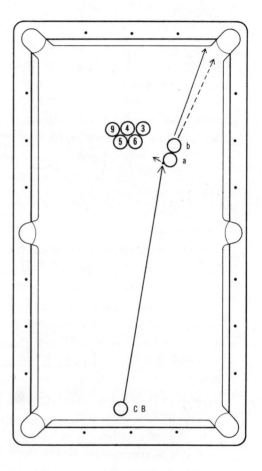

FIGURE 19A

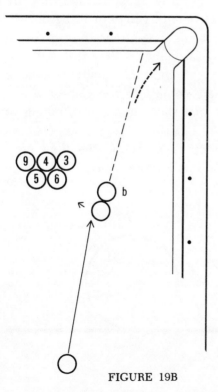

FIGURE 19B

Ball *b*, moving from left to right, has the entire width of the pocket for a target area, plus an additional small area on the rail. Ball *b* "drifts" in an arc into the pocket.

The cue ball breaks the pack and rebounds into the safe area.

In all throw shots, it is wise to check and make sure that the balls are frozen. The meshing action and the energy passing through the frozen balls causes this changing of direction. But it is possible to throw balls that are not frozen, and I suggest that you work out for yourself the various distances which are possible for you and your stroke. As a rule, a separation of ¼ inch is about the limit. Thus, on a straight-on shot with almost a full face and a small space up to ¼ inch, it may be possible to get a throw, but not so much as when the balls are frozen. Also, by using English on the cue ball, you can get some results to help throw the second object ball.

The throw shot and combination shots have a number of advantages for the player. They not only offer an excellent way to break up the arrangement formed by their own positions but they often are the means of caroming the cue ball into the rack and spreading the balls so that it is easier to pick them off one by one.

I have gone into some detail with the throw shots because they are an essential part of the popular pocket billiard game. In 14.1 it is necessary to break the balls and clusters so as to continue the run. Once the rack has been disturbed, either by caroming off the break ball and opening the rack or by playing safety off the rack and thus opening spaces between the racked balls, there come into the game the elements of combinations, throw shots, kiss shots, and the caroming of one ball off another.

Later in this section we shall discuss these shots and give the secrets of how to make them, enumerating various ways in which a knowledge of them can be useful.

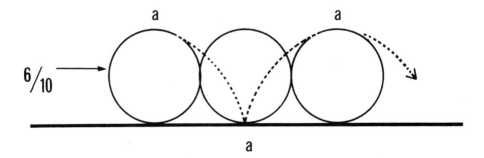

FIGURE 20

3

Perfect Rolling

WHEN THE CUE BALL is struck by the cue, it skids for a short distance and then begins normal rolling; that is, all parts of the circumference of the ball come in contact with the covering of the table.

If the cue ball is struck slightly above center (six-tenths of its height), it will attain perfect rolling quicker than when struck elsewhere. The cue must be held level, and the stroke must be smooth.

See drawing on facing page.

4

Imperfect Rolling

WHEN A BALL is struck by the cue above center, it rotates around the horizontal axis more times, in a given distance, than in normal rotation.

When a ball rotating in this fashion strikes another ball, there is a tendency for it to impart its energy to the second ball and then roll forward or follow the second ball because of this excessive spin.

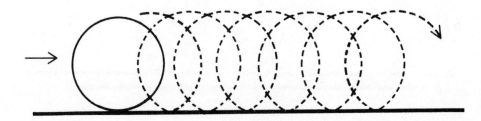

FIGURE 21

105

5

Follow Ball

TO HIT a follow ball (Fig. 22), keep the cue stick level with the table; stroke through the cue ball; and contact the cue ball above the center spot on the vertical axis.

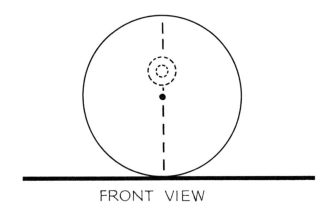

FRONT VIEW

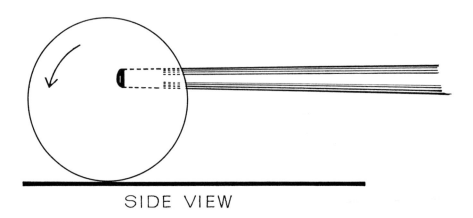

SIDE VIEW

FIGURE 22

Figure 23 shows how to control the follow ball so as to arrive at the desired objective: cue ball to hit object ball 1 and then travel in the desired path to object ball 2.

To achieve this effect, draw an imaginary line through the center of object ball 1 to object ball 2 and note spot I on the far side of object ball 1. Draw and aim the cue ball at this spot. The contact point of cue ball on object ball 1 will be at II, but the direction of cue ball will be to object ball 2.

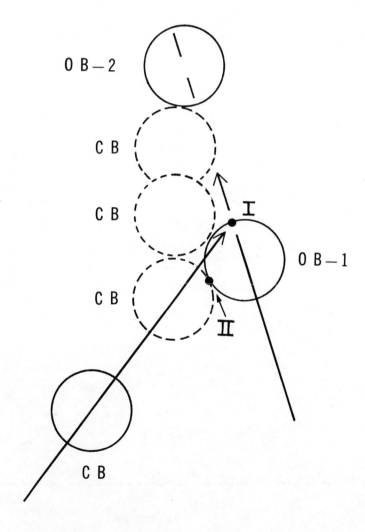

O B — 2

C B

C B

I

O B — 1

C B

II

C B

FIGURE 23

To arrive at point of aim in Figure 24, sight through the centers of object balls 1 and 2.

Aim center of cue ball at point of aim on far side of object ball. Use level cue and hit the cue ball above center on the vertical axis. Use moderate speed.

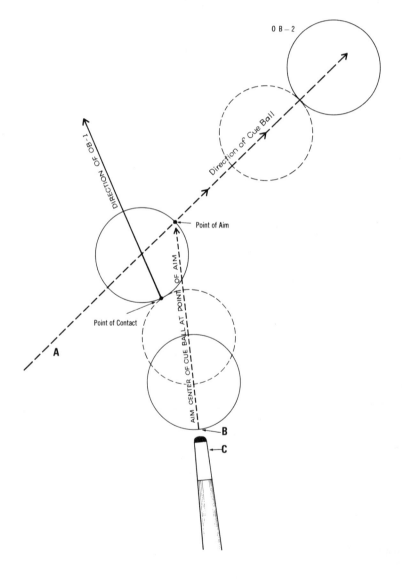

FIGURE 24

To make a follow shot with English on the cue ball (Fig. 25), note the following:

A normal hit at point of aim (without using English) would result in object ball 1 striking object ball 2.

But using right side English puts spin on the cue ball and throws object ball 1 into a left path, away from object ball 2.

Aim the cue ball at the point of aim, using moderate speed.

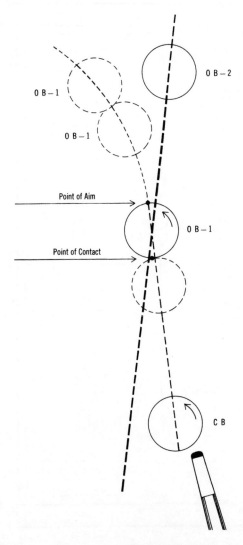

FIGURE 25

Figure 26 illustrates the effect of speed on the cue ball as it contacts the object ball. (All of these strokes use the same contact point on the cue ball.)

Heavy line indicates moderate speed on the cue ball.

Cue ball follows path (1) if struck with too much power or speed; cue ball follows path (2) if power is most excessive.

Hit the cue ball one cue-tip width above center on the vertical axis.

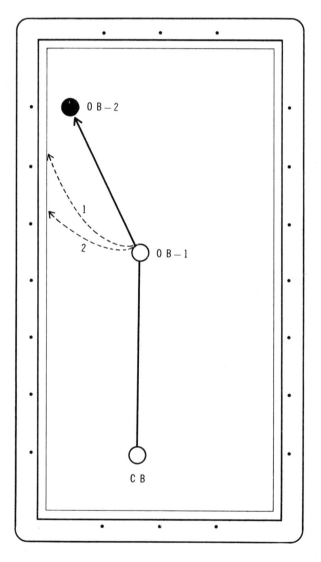

FIGURE 26

Here are two examples of the correct amount of speed (Fig. 27).

A. Object balls 1 and 2 are about two feet apart.

Use a soft stroke just sufficient to carry the cue ball to object ball 2 and a little beyond; use regular follow bridge; stroke the cue ball one cue-tip width above center on the vertical axis.

B. Cue ball and object ball are about six inches apart.

Use "nip follow" stroke and a short bridge.

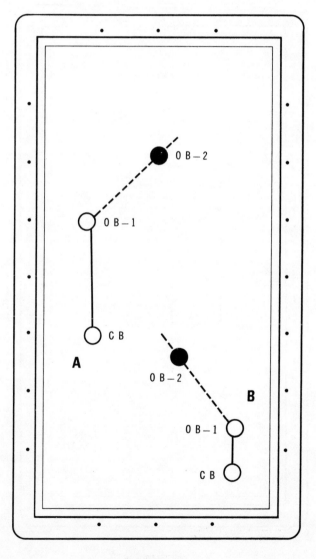

FIGURE 27

Figure 28 shows the effects of power and English applied to the cue ball in changing its direction from object ball 1 to object ball 2, 2*a*, 2*b*.

Note that increased speed on the cue ball and more right-hand English alters the angle off of object ball 1.

The next three diagrams show the effects of follow on the cue ball at various distances.

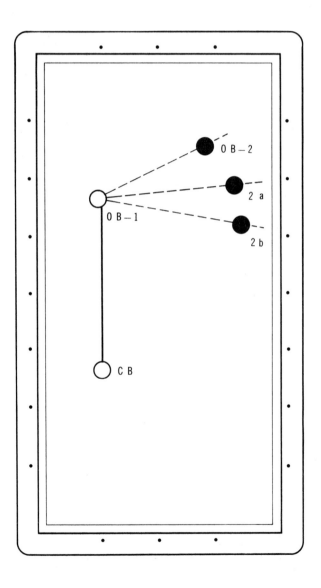

FIGURE 28

At a normal distance of one to two feet, cue ball to object ball 1 (Fig. 29):

Use moderate speed to carry cue ball to object ball 2; strike cue ball one cue-tip width above center on vertical axis.

The dotted line represents the actual path of the cue ball after striking object ball 1.

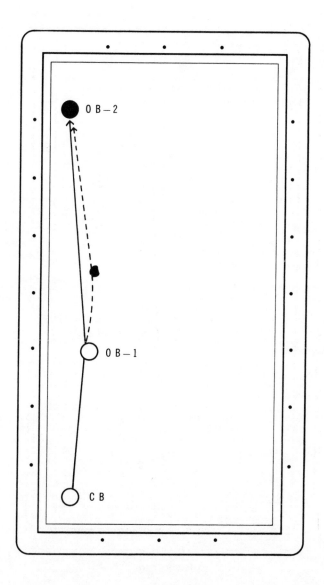

FIGURE 29

In Figure 30, object ball 1 is 4 to 7 feet away from the cue ball.

It is not advisable to play this shot as in Figure 29, although it can be made that way.

Instead, strike the cue ball *below* center, with full forward thrust. Moderate but not excessive power should be used.

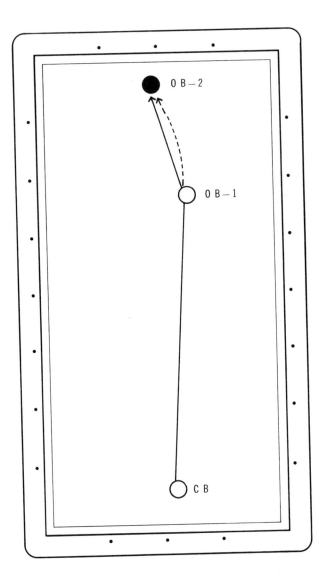

FIGURE 30

ADVANCED SHOTS

When the cue ball is near the object ball (4 to 8 inches), as in Figure 31, the normal follow bridge cannot be used.

To avoid fouling the balls, use a nip follow bridge; use a short, snappy stroke above center; and hold cue level.

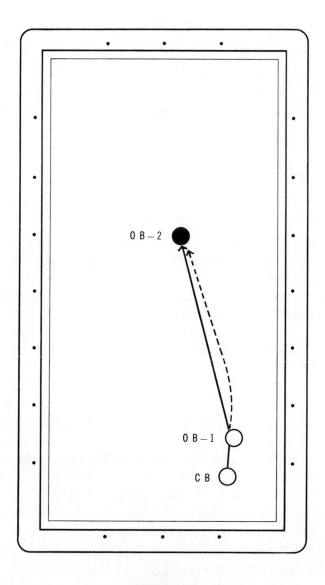

FIGURE 31

6

The Draw Shot

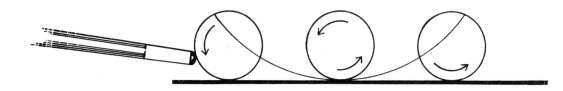

FIGURE 32

A BALL struck below the center of the horizontal axis by the cue stick revolves with a backward motion. Upon contact with the object ball, the cue ball imparts forward motion to the object ball. However, the excessive reverse spin catches the felt, causing the cue ball to rotate backwards.

In order to achieve this effect, use a slightly inclined cue and strike the ball below the center with a springy motion.

USE OF THE DRAW BALL IN HITTING THE TARGET

The problem in Figure 33 is for the cue ball to hit object ball 1 and object ball 2.

To execute this shot perfectly, draw an imaginary line through the center of cue ball 1 to object ball 1, and then draw another imaginary line through the center of object ball 1 to object ball 2.

Bisect this angle, and you get aim point I. Direct the cue ball at this aim point, using draw, and it will travel to object ball 2.

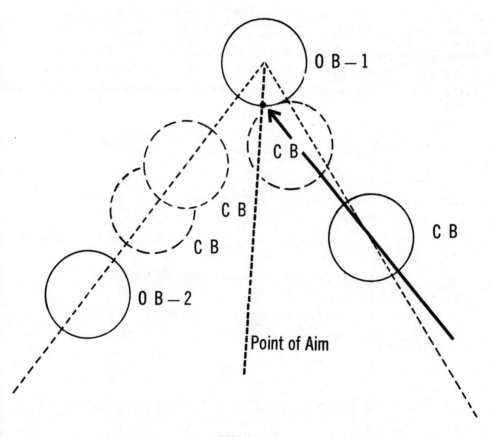

FIGURE 33

Figure 34 shows two draw shots. As we have seen, to make regular draw shot A, bisect the angle formed by imaginary lines drawn between the centers of the three balls and aim the center of the cue ball at spot on the edge of object ball 1 determined by bisecting the angle.

Use moderate speed; make a center ball hit one cue-tip width below center spot; hold cue level.

The cue ball takes the path of the dotted line to object ball 2.

When the cue ball lies very near object ball 1, as in B, bisect the angle and aim at the center spot, as in Figure 34.

Bring bridge hand close to the cue ball, with fingers drawn in and bridge firm; use nip draw, snappy wrist action, and moderate power; hold cue level or slightly elevated.

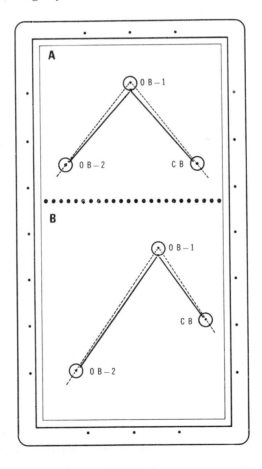

FIGURE 34

When object ball 1 is near the rail, a cue ball struck with top or center English often takes an erratic path (shown by the dotted line in Figure 35), because the cue ball pulls against itself as it reverses direction.

If the cue ball is struck *low*, it has forward direction with reverse spin. As the cue ball strikes the rail and changes direction, the reverse spin complements this direction, and the result is a truer path for the cue ball.

When low right English is used on the cue ball, it strikes object ball 1, returns to the rail, and rebounds to the left. This is very important for position play. (Fig. 36).

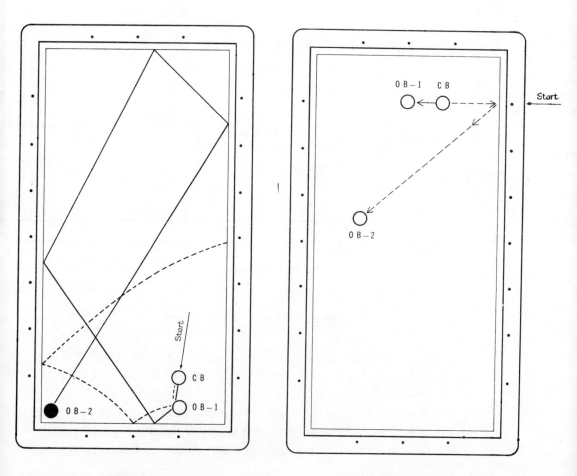

FIGURE 35   FIGURE 36

CUE BALL REBOUND

The use of English on the cue ball affects the angle of rebound from the rails.

Right English on the cue ball, as in Figure 37, causes the ball to reverse itself as it comes off the rails. The angle opens off the first rail, closes off the second rail, and opens off the third rail.

Left English on the cue ball would close the angle off the first rail, open it off the second rail, and close it off the third rail.

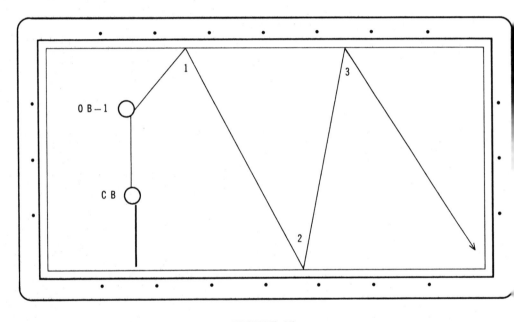

FIGURE 37

OBJECT BALL REBOUND

In Figure 38, a cue ball hit with left-hand English is driven into the object ball, throwing it into the rail with imparted English. (Left English on the cue ball throws the object ball to the right.)

The object ball opens the angle off the first rail (1), closes the angle off the second rail (2), and opens the angle off the third rail (3).

The reverse is true of a cue ball hit with right-hand English.

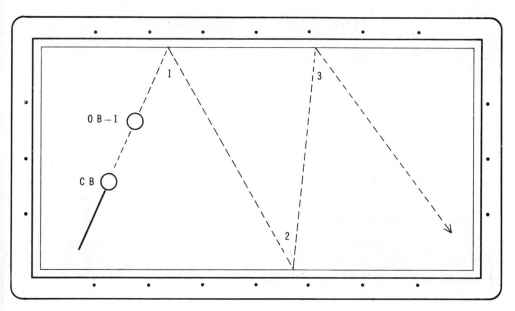

FIGURE 38

With no English on the cue ball, and a moderate stroke—and where (1) equals the angle of incident and (2) equals the angle of reflection or rebound—the rebound angle and the angle of incident are equal (Fig. 39).

If you use a strong forward thrust, you close the angle; if you use a soft forward thrust, you open the angle.

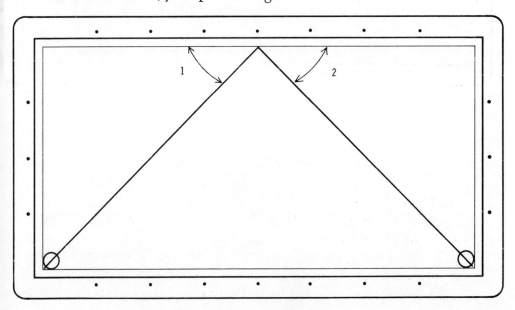

FIGURE 39

7

The Piquet

THE PIQUET is a draw shot which goes forward and then reverses direction without striking an object ball. The backward spin imparted to the cue ball is greater than the forward thrust and overcomes friction forward.

To make the piquet shot, use an inclined cue (see Figure 40) and the draw stroke.

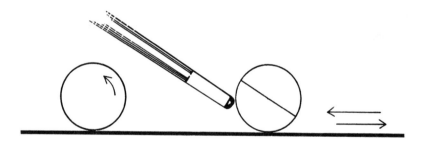

FIGURE 40

8

The Massé

THE MASSÉ is a professional shot not recommended for beginners. The cue ball is struck with a sharp downward stroke of the cue, as shown in Figure 41.

A close massé is made with the angle of inclination of the downward stroke between 78 and 80 degrees.

A half massé calls for an angle of 68 to 70 degrees.

A long massé calls for an angle of 48 to 50 degrees.

A jump massé calls for an angle of 25 to 60 degrees.

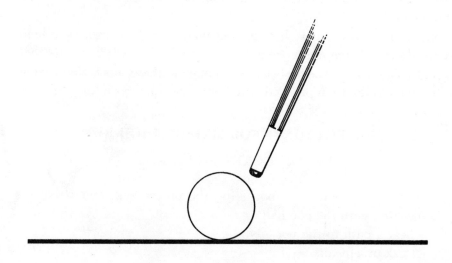

FIGURE 41

9

Break Shots

FOR continuous runs in 14.1 pocket billiards, the key to success lies in the key ball, or the fourteenth ball of the run. This is the last ball taken off the table before the balls are racked again. Select as the key ball one which, when pocketed, will leave the cue ball in such position that the distance to the *break ball*, or the fifteenth ball of the run, is short (2 or 3 feet) and the angle off the break ball is not difficult. Then concentrate on the amount of spin and speed to be used to bring the cue ball away from the rack—either by employing draw or forward forcing follow—so it will contact a rail and move toward the center of the table before the scattering balls interfere with it. Occasionally, when the angle warrants it, the player may elect to hit the rack with a dead ball in order to scatter the cluster and leave the cue ball stationary.

Experiment with break shots in continuous practice sessions to help yourself develop immunity from impact noise and the latent fears that seem to plague even the best players in making these shots. Know what you intend to do; then proceed with confidence in your ability to do it.

STRATEGY HINTS FOR MAKING HIGH RUNS
IN 14.1 POCKET BILLIARDS

1. Strive for accuracy in pocketing the object ball, and strive for position with the cue ball.
2. Clear a path to the pockets.
3. Break up clusters.
4. Pocket balls near the rail.
5. Keep the cue ball away from the rails.
6. Select the key ball and break ball, but have alternates in reserve.
7. Use a soft stroke and control the cue ball.
8. Keep the distance from the cue ball to the object ball relatively short—1 to 3 feet.

9. As a general rule, it is better for the cue ball to be in the center of the table, rather than confined to the top or end zones.
10. Avoid "scratching" the cue ball.

SECRET OF THE KEY BALL

The key ball is the fourteenth ball pocketed in 14.1 pocket billiards. It should be near a pocket and in a position which will permit the cue ball to deflect from it and come near the break ball.

Allow for an angle on the break ball in order to reopen the pack.

Figure 42 shows two shots: The pocketing of the key ball and the pocketing of the break ball after the fourteen balls have been reracked. The dotted lines show the path of the cue ball in pocketing the key ball, and the solid lines show the path of the cue ball and break ball.

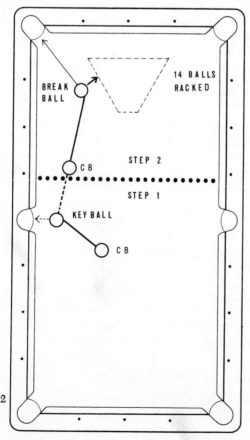

FIGURE 42

125

EXAMPLES OF BREAK SHOTS IN POCKET BILLIARDS

The dotted ball is the key ball. It is important to consider this ball, so as to get the best position and angle on the fifteenth ball.

Figure 43 shows a standard break. Best position: try to hit the last two balls.

Figure 44 is from back of the rack. You can carom off the called ball into the rack, then to Rail I, II, III, and out to center area of table.

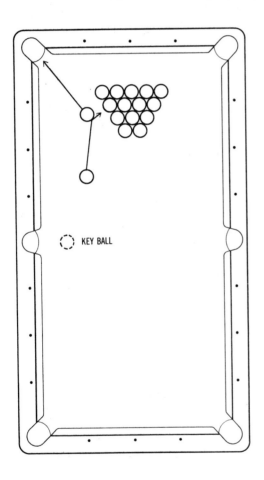

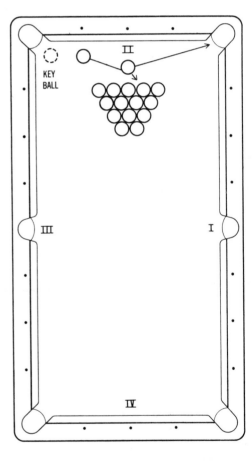

FIGURE 43   FIGURE 44

Figure 45 shows a side pocket break. Beware of scratching in end pocket.

Figure 46 is a head rail break. There are many other angles from the head rail—not the best, but not hopeless.

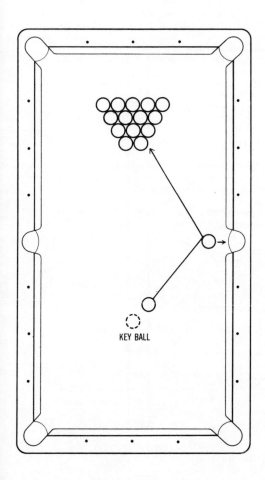

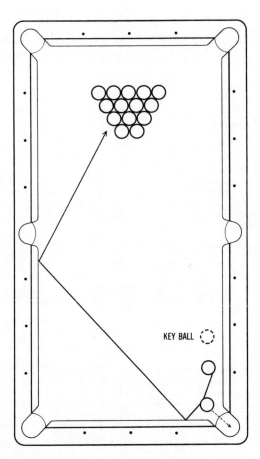

FIGURE 45

FIGURE 46

EXAMPLE OF A BREAK SHOT IN CAROM BILLIARDS

The red object ball is spotted at the foot spot, and opponent's white ball is on head spot.

The starting player is left or right of white object ball. He must contact red object ball first. Failure to do so ends his inning.

Subsequent shots can be attempted off either the red or white ball.

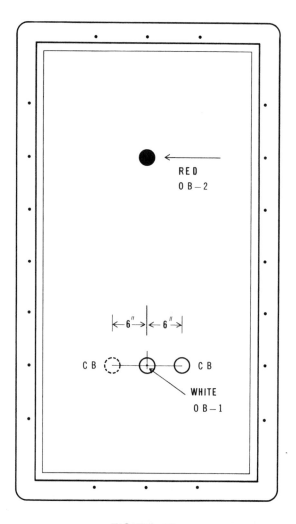

FIGURE 47

PART FOUR

The Diamond System
for Three-Cushion Billiards

1

Introductory Remarks

THE DIAMOND SYSTEM for Three-cushion Billiards is based upon a mathematical formula which will help the player in determining where to hit the first rail with the cue ball so that it gets on the correct track in its course around the table.

In this system the cue ball may strike the first object ball, go into the *first rail*, then to two or more rails, and then into the second object ball to score; or the cue ball may contact three or more rails and then contact the two object balls.

There are other ways of making points in three-cushion billiards, but the Diamond system does not apply to them.

For our purposes we have arranged the various steps in learning the system in an extended and explanatory way, so as to be as helpful as possible and to add to your enjoyment of billiards. Practice each step on the table and note the results, as you learn.

No system in billiards is perfect or even near perfect. There are too many variables and human factors to make one particular method entirely accurate.

Variables include the composition, age, size, shape, cleanliness, and elasticity of the balls; the size, balance, rail height, and covering (texture, age, warp-woof) of the table; the weight, straightness, elasticity, and type of wood of the cue; and the size, contour, type and abrasive quality of the cue tip.

As for the human factors, no two humans are alike in size, shape, temperament, and psychological make-up, or in creative ability, logical reasoning, memory aptitude, emotional control, or mental and muscular coordination.

The Diamond system is of help to the advanced player as a guide and a check upon his own reasoning. It is suggested that beginners learn the fundamentals of billiards, and that they play carom and straight rail, before they go on to three-cushion billiards.

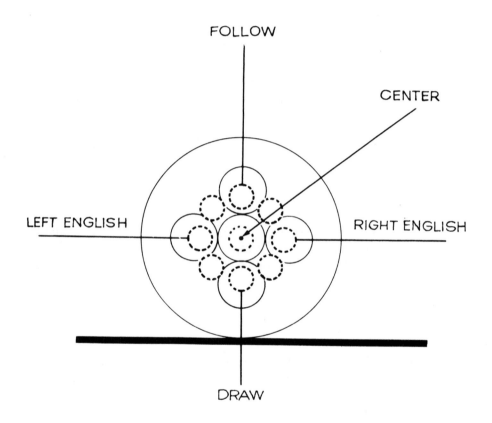

FIGURE 1

2

Advanced English

English, or spin, on the cue ball has an effect upon the cue ball (1) as it travels over the surface of the table, (2) as it hits the first object ball, (3) as it hits the rail, (4) as it progresses around the table, (5) as it is applied to open an angle (running) or close the angle (reverse English), (6) as it throws the object ball left or right as in pocket billiards, (7) in massé, caroms, balk-line, and three-cushion shots, (8) in piquet and jump shots, (9) in follow shots with imperfect rotation, and (10) in draw with imperfect rotation.

The amount of English depends upon the location on the cue ball where it is applied (see Fig. 1.), the amount of force of feathering applied with the cue (speed of stroke), and the level, elevated, or lowered position of the cue. The English is effective, moderate, or negligible, depending upon the various points of contact on the object ball. The English reacts differently as it goes into a rail at various angles (obtuse, right angle, acute). The English is smooth or erratic depending upon the stroke delivery and the abrasive action, or friction, of the cue tip upon the cue ball.

In practicing with Figure 1, confine shots to cue-tip width. Draw shots are hit slightly farther from the center than is the general rule.

Note the small circles, indicating areas used in professional play.

THREE EXAMPLES OF RUNNING ENGLISH

In Figure 2, the cue ball contacts the side rail, in this instance with left-hand English. Use moderate speed.

The lines denoting the path of the cue ball are drawn to the edge of the rails for clarity. The actual contact point of ball and rail is above the spot (see Fig. 13).

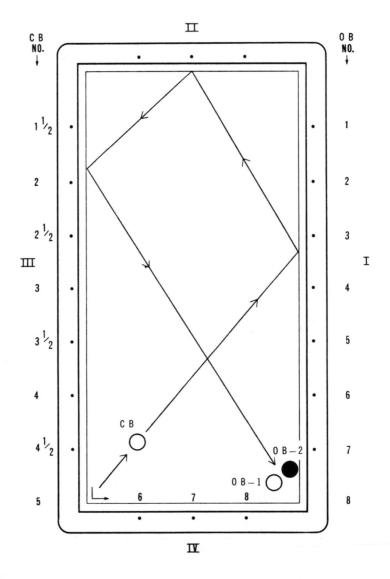

134   FIGURE 2

In Figure 3, the cue ball contacts object ball 1 on left side.

The cue ball hits object ball 1 with left-hand running English and moderate speed. The cue ball strikes the object ball on the left side and the cue ball goes to the left, spinning to the right in clockwise rotation, and continues the right rotation off the rail and opening the angle.

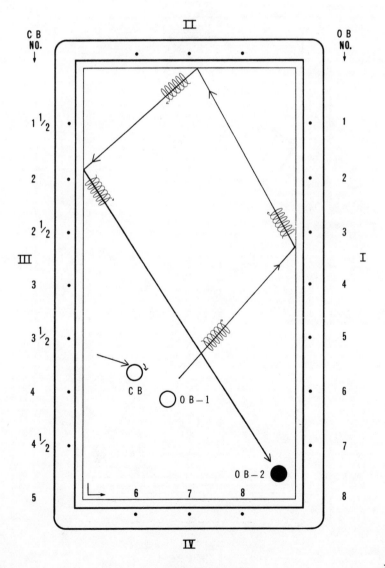

FIGURE 3

In Figure 4, cue ball contacts object ball 1 on the *right* side with *left* English on cue ball. Note right spin on cue ball as it deflects from OB-1 to direction of rails I, II, III.

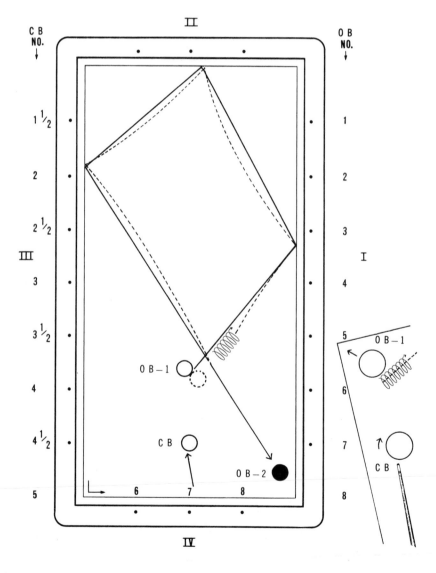

FIGURE 4

3

Cue Ball at Each Corner of the Table

In Figure 5, you are at the head of the table in the lower left-hand corner, and the rails are numbered from the top down. The rail opposite you is No. 1, and the ball travels counterclockwise around the table.

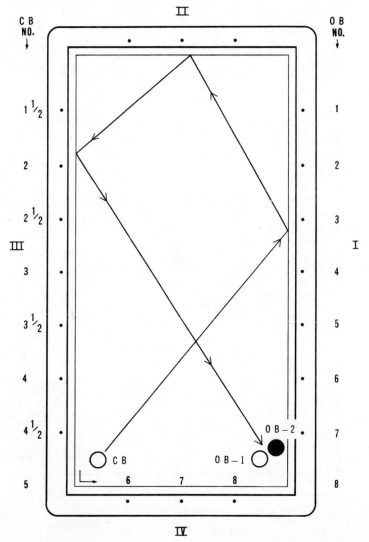

FIGURE 5

In Figure 6, you are at the head of the table in the lower right-hand corner, and the rails are numbered from the top down. The rail opposite you is No. 1, and the ball travels clockwise around the table.

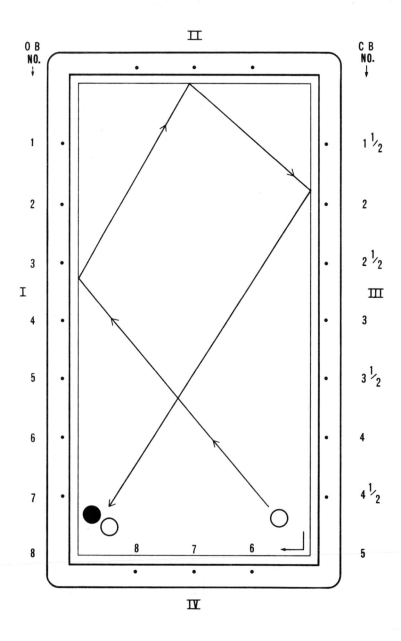

FIGURE 6

In Figure 7, you are at the foot of the table at the upper left-hand corner, and the rails are numbered from top (away from you) down; the ball travels clockwise around the table.

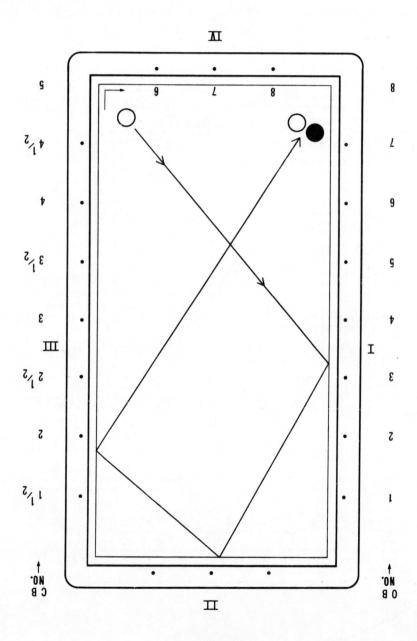

FIGURE 7

In Figure 8, you are at the foot of the table at the upper right-hand corner, and the rails are numbered from top (away from you) down; and the ball travels counterclockwise around the table.

The numbers on the opposite side are the object ball numbers. The numbers on the side near you are the cue ball numbers.

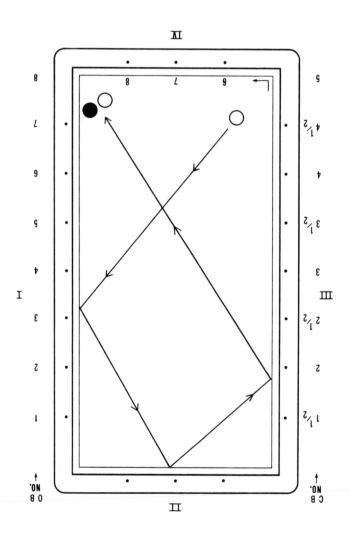

FIGURE 8

4

Cue Ball and Object Ball Numbers

Memorize the object ball numbers and the cue ball numbers in Figure 9. Note that the numbering always begins with lower numbers *away* from you and increases as they come toward you. Object ball numbers run from 1 to 7; cue ball numbers from 1 to 5 and 6, 7, 8, with cue ball numbers extending onto Rail IV because the table is twice as long as it is wide (generally 5 by 10 feet).

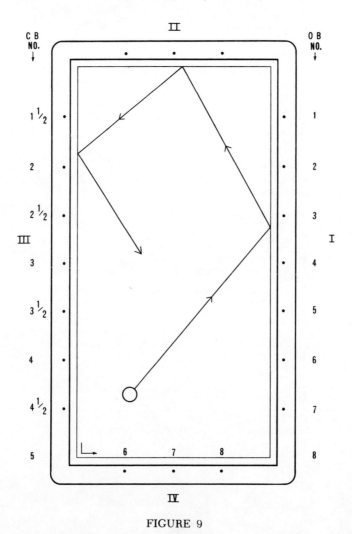

FIGURE 9

5

Cue Ball Tracks

Any ball on the track line is on the track of that number. Figure 10 shows three examples: cue ball numbers 4½, 5, and 6.

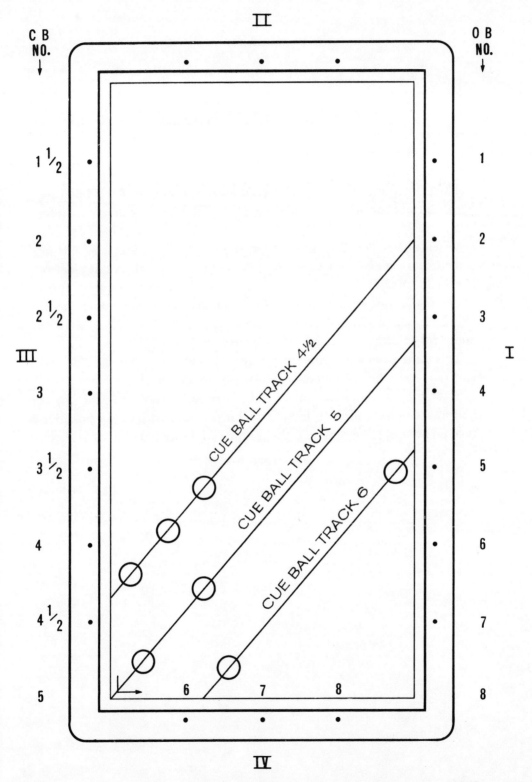

FIGURE 10

6

The "Big Ball" Principle

The principle of the big ball is very useful in three-cushion billiards, because the possibilities for scoring are multiplied considerably. Refer to Figure 11.

When object ball 2 is in a corner, the cue ball can score by hitting directly (A) on the left side, or in the center, or on the right side, or from left to right. This gives a target area of slightly less than three diameters, minus a fraction of an inch to allow for legal contact. If the cue ball and object ball are $2\frac{3}{8}$ inches across, $2\frac{3}{8} + 2\frac{3}{8} + 2\frac{3}{8}$ (to allow for contact) equals 7-9/64 inches target area.

This same principle applies when the cue ball comes off the side and end rails to strike the object ball, as in B, C, D, and E.

Since the cue ball can contact the fourth rail or fifth rail, the object ball in the corner offers quite a large target area, with many possibilities for scoring even when the regular anticipated way has been missed.

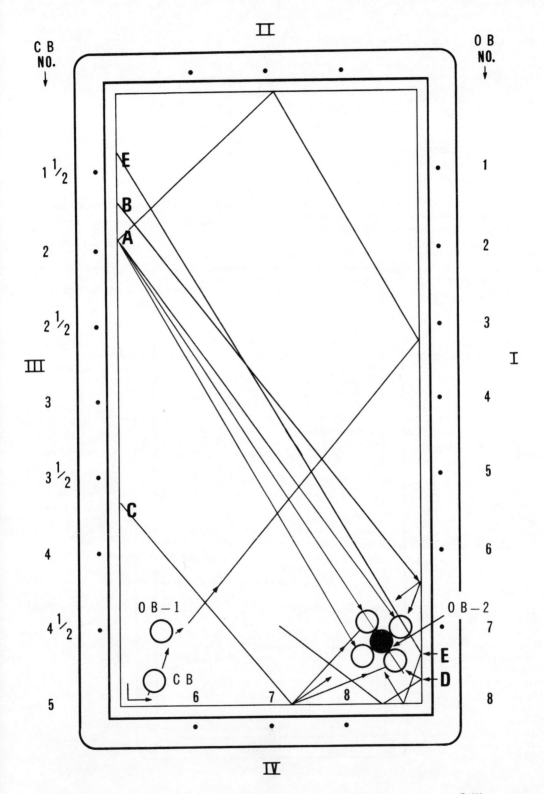

FIGURE 11

7

Shooting through the Spot

Many players erroneously aim at a point on the rail in line with the spot. Do not make this mistake.

Aim instead by shooting through the spot as shown. Note how the contact point on the rail (CP) varies with the different angles.

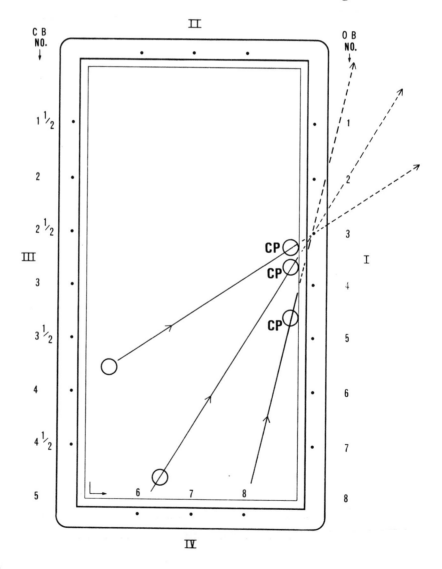

FIGURE 12

8

Cue Ball Contact Points

Figure 13 shows the actual path of the cue ball and its contact points on the rails. Use running English.

For clarity the lines are usually drawn directly to the rails (see Figure 2).

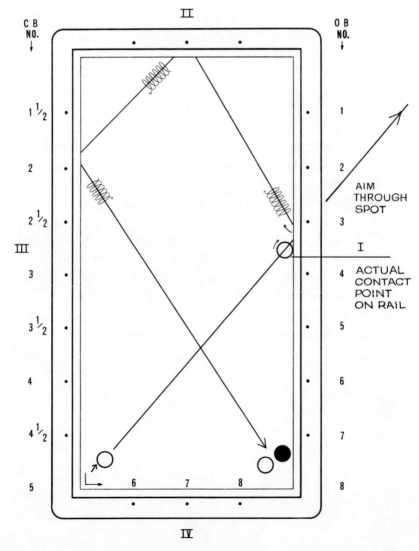

FIGURE 13

9

Third Rail to First Rail

Figure 14 illustrates the same situation as Figure 13 except that the lines are drawn to the points on the rail for clarity.

Study Figure 14. Memorize the track the cue ball takes off the third rail after it contacts Rails I and II.

A ball coming off the third rail in the top corner goes into Diamond No. 6 on the first rail.

A ball coming off the third rail at Diamond No. 1 goes into Diamond No. 7 on the first rail.

A ball coming off the third rail at Diamond No. 2 goes *into the corner* of Rail I.

A ball coming off the third rail at Diamond No. 3 goes to the end rail at 1 diamond space distance on end rail.

A ball coming off the third rail at Diamond No. 4 goes to the end rail—1¾ diamond distance from the right side.

This memorization is basic for all further computations.

Reasoning: I wish to have the cue ball go into the right-hand corner. I know that a ball coming off the third rail at Diamond No. 2 will go into the corner. The cue ball is on 5. Subtract 2 from 5 and the result is Diamond No. 3 on the first rail. Aim through Diamond No. 3 on the first rail; and the cue ball contacts that rail, the top rail, the third rail (at Diamond No. 2), and goes into the corner.

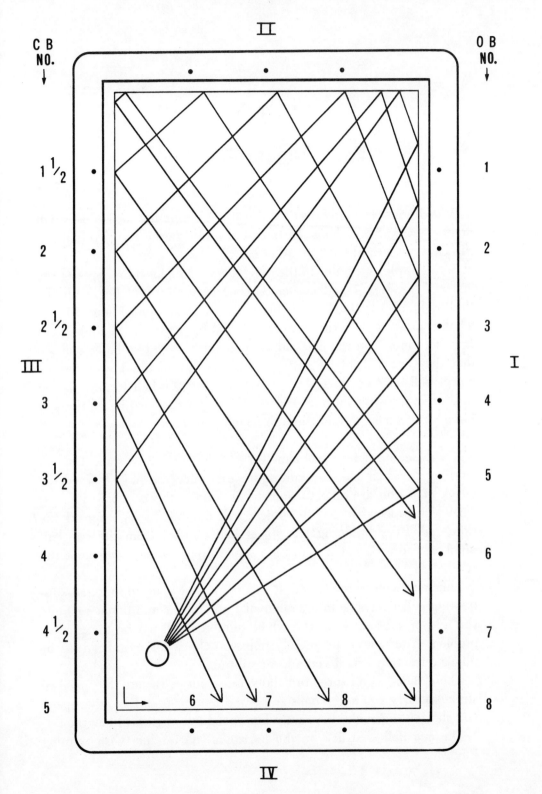

FIGURE 14

149

10

Sighting

With Figure 14 memorized, you can determine the near object ball number by walking along the third rail and sighting the two balls, in this case (or a single ball, in other cases).

For example, in Figure 15 the two balls are in a location opposite the first rail between 7 and corner 8. Your reasoning will begin on the third rail and work back to the first rail. You know from Figure 14 that a ball coming off 1 on the third rail after it has caromed off Rails I and II will go into 7 on the first rail. As you sight these two balls, you see that they are ¾ distance past 7. You add this to the 1 and set the object ball total of 1¾. You already know the cue ball location is (in this case) 5, so you subtract 1¾ from 5 and get the location on the first rail of 3¼. This is the spot through which you shoot.

If you set up a few problems for yourself and take some time in working out each one, you will notice that once you have learned the knack of it you are able to quickly determine the cue ball number. Then you proceed to get the object ball number by sighting off the third rail. By subtracting the object ball number from the cue ball number, you arrive at the location spot through which you shoot the cue ball.

This may seem complicated at this point, but your adding and subtracting will always be in the range of 1 and 8. The additional amounts you add or subtract from the whole numbers will not be too great a problem. Your reasoning merely tells you the whole number plus or minus a fraction which you add or subtract.

These shots, as all three rail shots, are made with just the speed of stroke to carry you to the balls and 3 or 4 feet beyond. Excessive speed will shorten the angle. If you use less speed the angle will lengthen.

The cue ball is struck on the horizontal center line with running English.

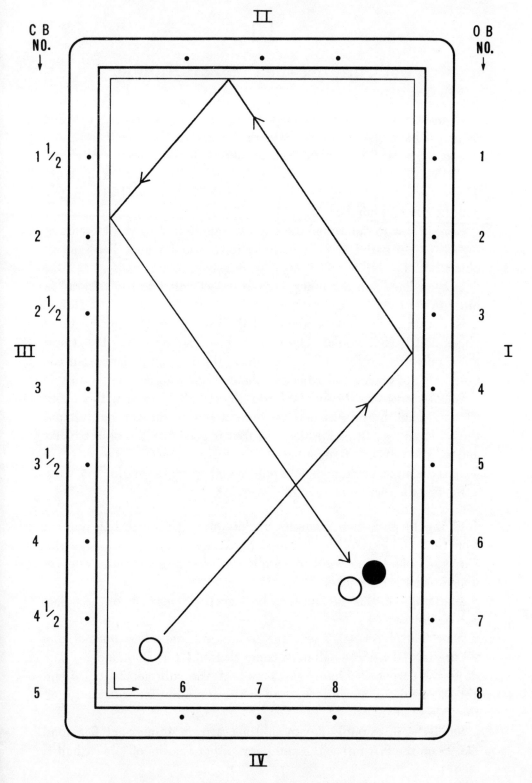

C B
NO.

O B
NO.

1 ½

1

2

2

2 ½

3

III

I

3

4

3 ½

5

4

6

4 ½

7

5

6   7   8   8

IV

FIGURE 15

11

Determining the Cue Ball Number

In most three-cushion shots your cue ball must contact the first object ball and then the three rails to the second object ball.

You might well ask, at this point, "Where is the cue ball number?" or, "How do I determine the cue ball number for this type of shot?" The answer is quite simple. The edge of the first object ball will give you the cue ball number.

Here is how to determine the cue ball number when you are caroming off object ball 1 to go into Rails I, II, and III and then contact object ball 2:

Draw a line from the inner edge of object ball 1 to the side rail in order to get the cue ball number.

Note that you do not use the cue ball location but the inner edge of object ball 1 when you are caroming the cue ball off object ball 1 and three rails into object ball 2. You draw the imaginary line from the inner edge of object ball 1 back to the cue ball number.

When you stroke the cue ball into object ball 1, do so with smooth running English and just enough speed to carry the cue ball around the table, hitting three cushions, so that it goes into the object ball 2 and a little beyond. Remember that excessive speed on the cue ball lessens the angle off the rail, and mild speed opens the angle.

Review the section on caroms, pages 91ff.

Figure 16 gives two examples of determining the cue ball number from the inner edge of the first object ball.

In example A, the cue ball number is 5 because the inner edge of object ball 1 is on track 5.

In example B, the cue ball is 4½ because the inner edge of the object ball is on track 4½.

Note that object ball 2 is in the corner. We know from memorizing Figure 14 that the cue ball must come off Rail III at Diamond No. 2 to go to the corner. Therefore in example A you subtract 2 from 5 and get Diamond No. 3 on the first rail as the aim point for your carom off the object ball 1.

Similarly, in example B you subtract 2 from 4½ and get Diamond No. 2½ on the first rail as the aim point of your carom off object ball 1.

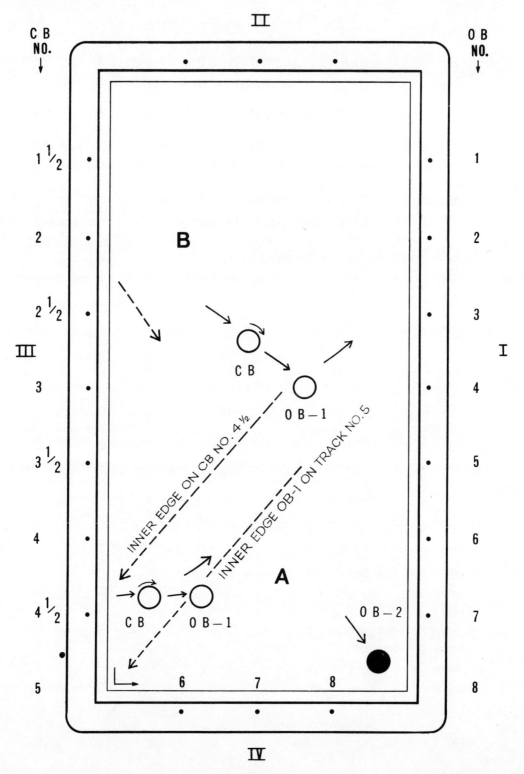

FIGURE 16

153

NINE PROBLEMS

IN DETERMINING THE CUE BALL NUMBER

Figure 17 illustrates how to determine the aim spot on the first rail when the object balls are in the lower right-hand corner and the cue ball is at 4½.

We know from memorization that the cue ball must come off the third rail at 2 in order to go into the corner. Therefore subtract 2 from 4½, and the aim point becomes 2½ on the first rail. Use moderate speed and running English on the stroke.

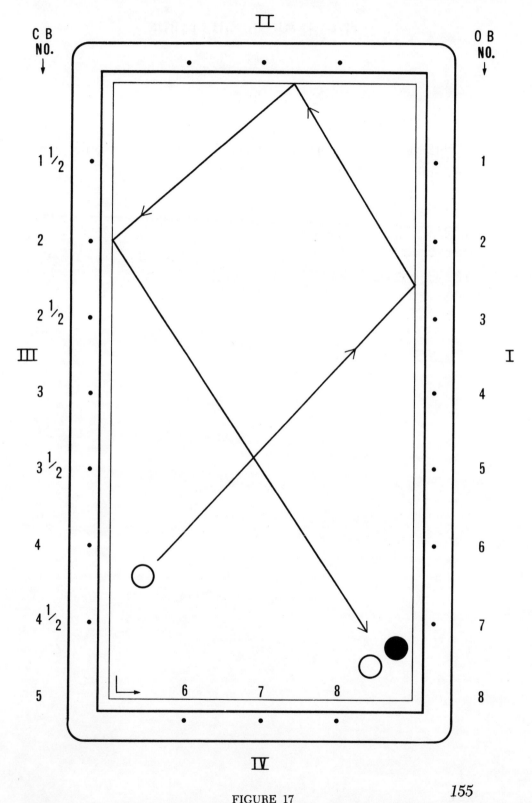

C B
NO.

O B
NO.

1 ½   1

2   2

2 ½   3

III   I

3   4

3 ½   5

4   6

4 ½   7

5   8

6   7   8

IV

FIGURE 17

With the cue ball at 4 and the object balls in the same corner, subtract 2 from 4 and aim at 2 on the first rail.

II

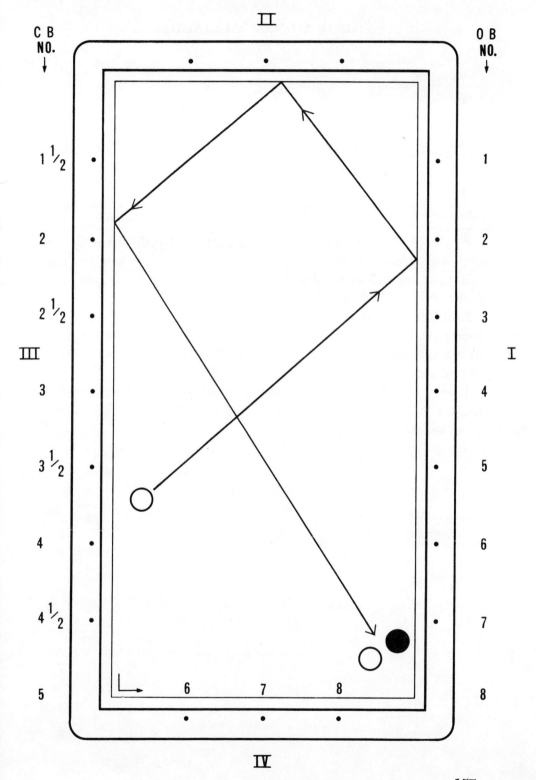

C B
NO.

O B
NO.

1 1/2   1

2   2

2 1/2   3

III   I

3   4

3 1/2   5

4   6

4 1/2   7

5   8

6   7   8

IV

FIGURE 18

157

As the cue ball moves down the rail past the fourth diamond, the angle changes somewhat because the table is twice as long as it is wide. The cue ball strikes the end rail more to the right and goes a bit past Diamond No. 2 on the third rail.

Realizing this, you compensate for the change by, here, altering your mathematics. In this instance, with the cue ball at 3½ you subtract 2 and get an aim point of 1½ on the first rail. However you actually hit slightly above 1½.

Each table has its own individuality, but you can determine the amount to add to your calculations by testing these shots before the game commences.

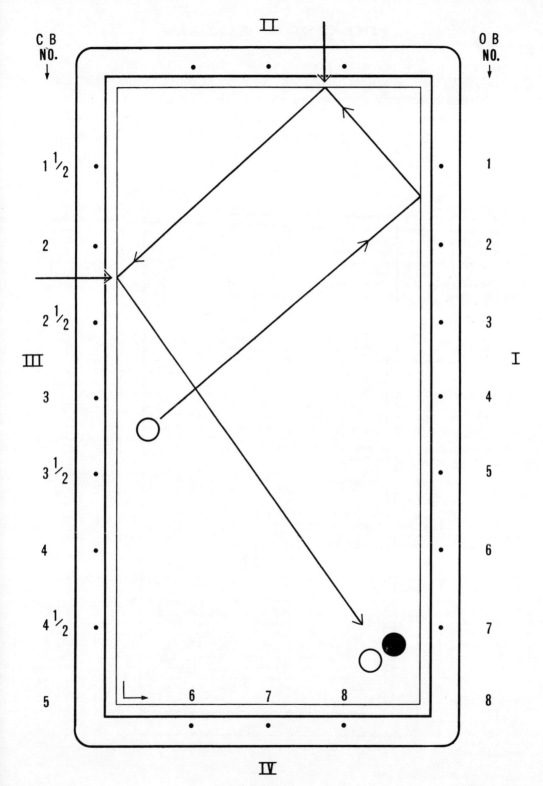

FIGURE 19

With the cue ball on 3, note that the point of contact on the third rail is slightly above 2 and the aim point on the first rail is at 1.

You must compensate, as in the previous illustration, for this added distance, by using a stroke with running English and moderate speed.

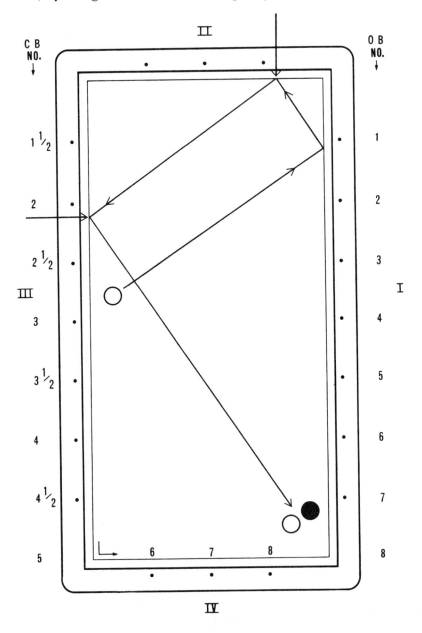

FIGURE 20

With the cue ball on 2½, note that the point of contact on the third rail is slightly more above 2, and the aim point on the first rail is at ½.

You must compensate, as before, using running English and moderate speed.

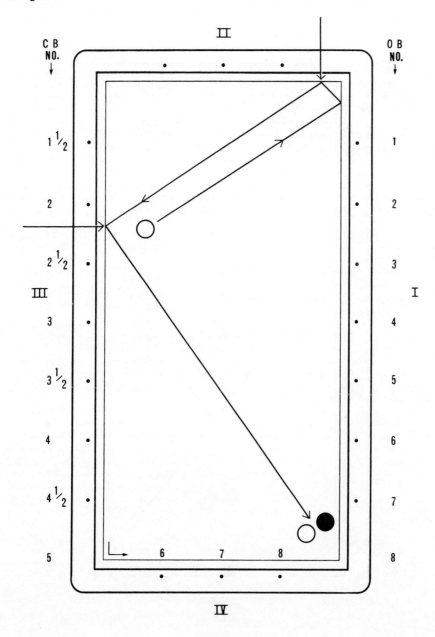

FIGURE 21

With the cue ball on 2, you must make a corner shot as shown in order to compensate and strike point *a* still farther up from 2 on the second rail, still using running English and moderate speed.

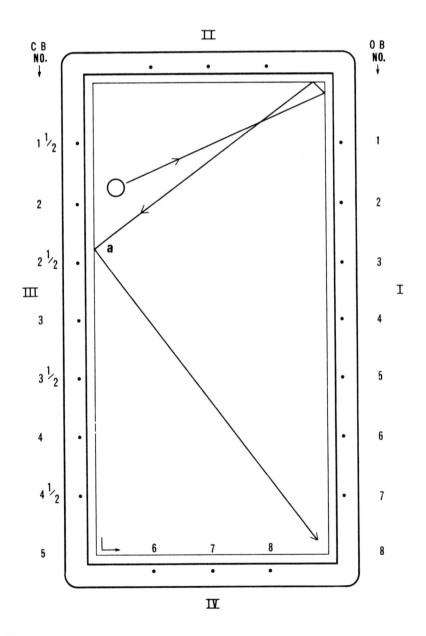

FIGURE 22

In the following three figures, the cue ball is moved along the end rail from the corner spot at 5 to 6, 7, and 8.

With the cue ball at 6, as in Figure 23, the aim point on the first rail becomes 6 minus 2, or 4. Compensate slightly for the acute angle on the first rail by using running English and moderate speed.

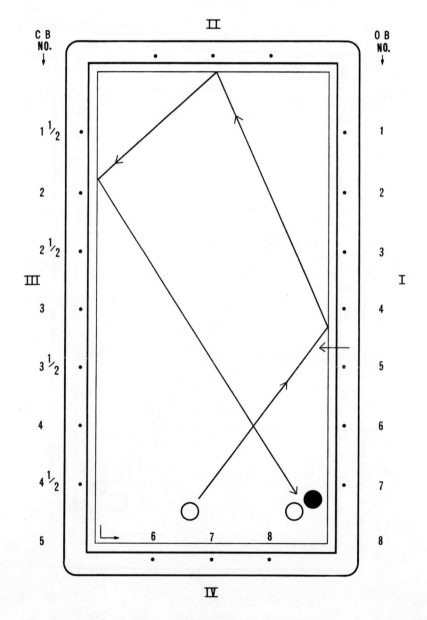

FIGURE 23

163

With the cue ball at 7, the aim point on the first rail becomes 5. Compensate for the acute angle.

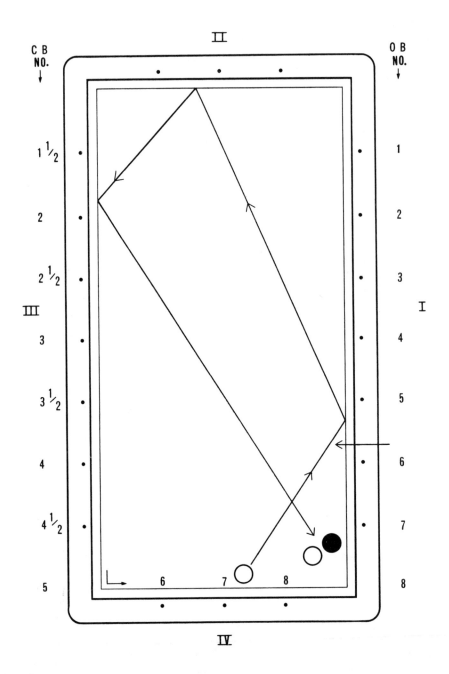

FIGURE 25

With the cue ball at 8, the aim point on the first rail is at 6. Compensate for the acute angle on Rail I.

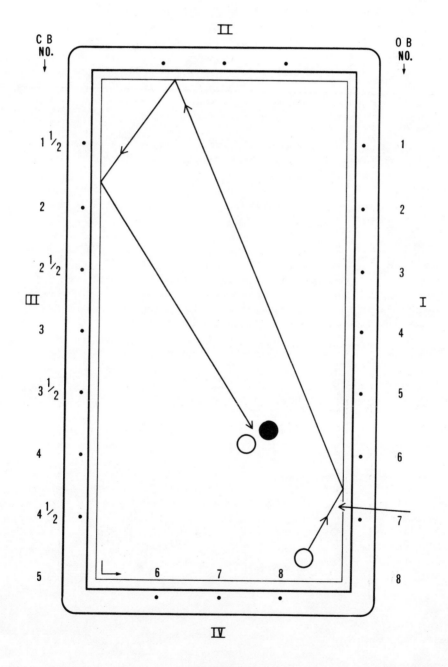

FIGURE 24